The Battle Of Passchendaele

Australian Army Campaigns Series – 28

Ian Finlayson

16pt

Copyright Page from the Original Book

© Copyright Army History Unit
Campbell Park Offices (CP2-5-166)
Canberra ACT 2600
AUSTRALIA
(02) 6266 4248
(02) 6266 4044 - fax
Copyright 2020 © Commonwealth of Australia

First published 2020

This book is copyright. Apart from any fair dealing for the purposes of private study, research, criticism or review as permitted under the Copyright Act, no part may be reproduced, stored in a retrieval system or transmitted in any form or by any means, electronic, mechanical, photocopying, recording or otherwise, without written permission.

The views expressed in this publication are those of the author(s) and not necessarily those of the Australian Army or the Department of Defence. The Commonwealth of Australia will not be legally responsible in contract, tort or otherwise for any statement made in this publication.

All inquiries should be made to the publishers.
Big Sky Publishing Pty Ltd
PO Box 303, Newport, NSW 2106, Australia
Phone: 1300 364 611
Email: info@bigskypublishing.com.au
Web: www.bigskypublishing.com.au

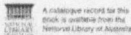
A catalogue record for this book is available from the National Library of Australia

Cover design and typesetting by Think Productions, Melbourne

Front cover and title page: In overcoats and newly issued socks, the men of the 10th Field Ambulance sit around the campfire scraping mud from their boots and clothes during a rest period at Dragoon Farm following the attack two days previously at Passchendaele Ridge (AWM E00945).

TABLE OF CONTENTS

LIST OF MAPS	i
MAP SYMBOLS	iii
SERIES INTRODUCTION	iv
ACKNOWLEDGEMENTS	v
LIST OF PERSONALITIES AND THEIR POSITIONS	vii
GLOSSARY AND ABBREVIATIONS	ix
INTRODUCTION	xiv
CHAPTER 1: PASSCHENDAELE: THE OPERATIONAL BACKGROUND TO THE BATTLE	1
CHAPTER 2: THE 3RD AUSTRALIAN DIVISION AND ALLIED OFFENSIVE TACTICS IN 1917	60
CHAPTER 3: THE 195TH GERMAN INFANTRY DIVISION AND GERMAN DEFENSIVE TACTICS IN 1917	88
CHAPTER 4: PASSCHENDAELE I: PLANNING THE 3RD AUSTRALIAN DIVISION'S ATTACK	119
CHAPTER 5: PASSCHENDAELE I: THE 3RD AUSTRALIAN DIVISION'S ATTACK	159
CHAPTER 6: PASSCHENDAELE II: THE CANADIAN CORPS ATTACK	236
CHAPTER 7: CONCLUSION: THE 3RD AUSTRALIAN DIVISION AT PASSCHENDAELE I	258
BIBLIOGRAPHY	289
BACK COVER MATERIAL	306
Index	309

LIST OF MAPS

Map 1 The topography of the Ypres area in 1917 showing its significance as a road, rail and canal communications hub.

Map 2 The outline of Haig's plan for the Flanders campaign as provided to General Petain on 18 May 1917.

Map 3 The Allied gains at the Battle of Messines, 7—14 June 1917.

Map 4 The extent of the advance of Gough's Fifth Army following the initial attack on 31 July 1917 and the subsequent attack on Langemarck on 16 August 1917.

Map 5 Ground captured by Plumer's Second Army during the battles of Menin Road, Polygon Wood, Broodseinde and Poelcappelle up to 9 October 1917.

Map 6 The German defensive lines in Flanders July 1917 prior to the commencement of the Third Ypres offensive.

Map 7 Map outlining the wet and marshy areas around Passchendaele village in late October 1917.

Map 8 Some of the identified German 195th Infantry Divisions barbed wire and defensive positions in the immediate surrounds of Passchendaele.

Map 9 Original map dated 9 October 1917 showing the three stages and objectives for the attack (Red, Blue and Green lines), corps boundaries and the proposed artillery barrage lines.

Map 10 Location of the 3rd Australian Division and flanking brigades on 12 October 1917, prior to the attack.

Map 11 Original map dated 9 October 1917 and showing the 10th Brigade boundary and the alphabetical areas each battalion in the brigade was responsible for clearing during the Passchendaele attack.

Map 12   Original map showing 'K' Track and Jack Track leading to the new front line on 16 October 1917.

Map 13   Allied dispositions at noon on 12 October 1917.

Map 14   Original map of the 9th Field Ambulance system of medical evacuation showing the RAPs and relay stations in support of the 9th Infantry Brigade on 12 October 1917.

Map 15   The Canadian attacks on Passchendaele from 26 October to 10 November 1917.

Map 16   The extent of the Allied advance in the Third Ypres campaign, commencing with the Battle of Messines on 7 June 1917 and concluding with the attacks by the Canadian Corps on 10 November 1917.

MAP SYMBOLS

MAP SYMBOLS

MILITARY

- ■ Australia and its Allies
- ■ Enemy
- ⊠ Infantry
- xxxxx Army Group
- xxxx Army
- xxx Corps
- xx Division
- x Brigade
- III Regiment
- II Battalion
- •• Platoon
- • Section

- ═══ Front Line
- ─── Objective (Red, Green, etc.)
- ─── Military Boundary
- ➤ Unit Deployment
- ∿∿∿ Trenches
- ↑N North

GEOGRAPHIC

COUNTRY

DISTRICT/PROVINCE

Natural Features

- ★ Capital City
- • City/Town
- ▪ Structure
- ∼ RIVER
- ▰ LAKE
- ⋯ CANAL
- Track
- ─── Road
- ┼┼┼ Railway line
- ▨ Elevated ground
- ▨ Woods
- ♨ Wet and Marshy Area

SERIES INTRODUCTION

In 2004, the then Chief of Army's Strategic Advisory Group, the Australian Army's senior generals, established a scheme to promote the study and understanding of military history within the Army. The focus was the Army's future generation of leaders and, from this, the Campaign Series was created. The series is intended to complement the Army's other history publications which are major analytical works of high quality, academically rigorous and referenced.

The Campaign Series focuses on leadership, command, strategy, tactics and personal experiences of war. Each title within the series includes extensive visual sources of information—maps, including specifically prepared maps in colour and 3D, commissioned artwork, photographs and graphics.

Covering major campaigns and battles, as well as those less known, the Australian Army History Unit's Campaign Series provides a significant contribution to the history of the Australian Army and an excellent introduction to its campaigns and battles.

Tim Gellel
Head, Australian Army History Unit

ACKNOWLEDGEMENTS

This book is dedicated to my grandfather, Private J.R. Finlayson, a member of the 59th Battalion, AIF, and survivor of the battles of Fromelles, Bullecourt, Polygon Wood, Villers-Bretonneux, Amiens and St Quentin Canal.

The idea for this book was instigated by the previous Head of the Australian Army History Unit, Dr Roger Lee, as part of a series to cover all the major battles involving the Australian Army in the First World War. Many people assisted in the production of this volume, but none more than my fellow historians in the Australian Army History Unit, Dr Andrew Richardson and Mr Nick Anderson. Both provided their invaluable assistance and insights into the processes associated with producing this book and it would not have been published without their assistance. Thanks should also go to those who read this manuscript and provided invaluable suggestions including Dr Roger Lee, Mr Nick Anderson, Mr Richard Pelvin, Ms Grace Finlayson and Lieutenant Colonel Kon Iliadis. My sincere appreciation also goes to the editor of this book, Mrs Cathy McCullagh. Without Cathy's diligence, guidance and eye for detail, this book would have been a diminished work. Thanks also to Denny Neave and the team at Big Sky Publishing for the production of this high-quality volume. Finally, many thanks to Mr Bill Frost who, at very short notice, agreed to take some photographs around Passchendaele village during a visit to France.

LIST OF PERSONALITIES AND THEIR POSITIONS

The British Government

David Lloyd George	British Prime Minister
Winston Churchill	First Lord of the Admiralty
Admiral John Jellicoe	First Sea Lord

The British Expeditionary Force

Field Marshal Sir John French	Commander of the British Expeditionary Force before being replaced by Haig in December 1915
Field Marshal Sir Douglas Haig	Commander of the British Expeditionary Force from December 1915 until the end of the war. Haig was the architect of the Third Ypres campaign.
Brigadier General John Charteris	Haig's Chief of Intelligence
Lieutenant Colonel Macmullen	Member of Haig's Headquarters Staff (Operations)
Lieutenant General Sir Hubert Plumer	Commander of the British Second Army
Major General Charles Harington	Chief of Staff to Plumer
Lieutenant General Sir Henry Rawlinson	Commander of the British Fourth Army
Lieutenant General Sir Hubert Gough	Commander of the British Fifth Army

The French Government and Army

Alexandre Ribot	French Premier
Marshal Joseph Joffre	Commander-in-Chief of the French Army until relieved of command in December 1916
Marshal Robert Nivelle	Replaced Joffre as Commander-in-Chief of the French Army
General Philippe Pétain	Chief of the General Staff of the French Army who replaced Nivelle as Commander-in-Chief of the French Army in the spring of 1917

ANZAC Corps and New Zealand

Lieutenant General Sir William Birdwood	Commander of I ANZAC Corps, Second Army
Lieutenant General Sir Alexander Godley	Commander of II ANZAC Corps, Second Army
Major General Sir Andrew Russell	Commander of New Zealand Division, II ANZAC Corps

Australian Imperial Force

Major General John Monash	Commander of 3rd Australian Division, II ANZAC Corps
Brigadier General James Cannan	Commander of 11th Brigade, 3rd Australian Division
Brigadier General Walter McNicoll	Commander of 10th Brigade, 3rd Australian Division
Brigadier General Charles Rosenthal	Commander of 9th Brigade, 3rd Australian Division
Padre George Cuttriss	43rd Battalion Chaplain, 11th Brigade
Major Lyndhurst Giblin	Company Commander, 40th Battalion, 10th Brigade
Lieutenant Colonel Robert Henderson	Commanding Officer, 39th Battalion, 10th Brigade
Lieutenant Norman McNicol	Officer, C Company, 37th Battalion, 10th Brigade
Lieutenant Colonel John Milne	Commanding Officer, 36th Battalion, 9th Brigade
Captain Richard Gadd	Company Commander, C Company, 36th Battalion, 9th Brigade
Major Henry Carr	Company Commander, C Company, 35th Battalion, 9th Brigade
Major J. McDowell	Officer, 35th Battalion, 9th Brigade
Captain William Dixon	Company Commander, A Company, 35th Battalion, 9th Brigade
Sergeant George Burgess	At the time of the battle, a lance corporal in D Company, 35th Battalion, 9th Brigade
Private George Bain	Soldier, 35th Battalion, 9th Brigade
Lieutenant Colonel Ernst Martin	Commanding Officer, 34th Battalion, 9th Brigade
Major Walter Fry	Company Commander, A Company, 34th Battalion, 9th Brigade
Captain John Richardson	Company Commander, A Company, 34th Battalion, 9th Brigade
Lieutenant Colonel Leslie Morshead	Commanding Officer, 33rd Battalion, 9th Brigade

Canadian Corps

Lieutenant General Sir Arthur Currie	Commander of the Canadian Corps
Brigadier Edward Morrison	General Officer Commanding Royal Artillery, Canadian Corps

German Army

Field Marshal Eric von Falkenhayn	Chief of the General Staff of the German Army
Field Marshal Paul von Hindenburg	Replaced von Falkenhayn as Chief of the General Staff of the German Army in August 1916
General Erich Ludendorff	Quartermaster General to von Hindenburg
Field Marshal Crown Prince Rupprecht	Commander of Army Group Rupprecht
General Herman von Kuhl	Chief of Staff, Army Group Rupprecht

GLOSSARY AND ABBREVIATIONS

Allied Formation Terms	
AIF	Australian Imperial Force. Title of the all-volunteer force that Australia despatched overseas to assist Britain.
ANZAC	Australian and New Zealand Army Corps. In October 1917, II ANZAC Corps comprised the 3rd Australian Division, the New Zealand Division and the 66th and 49th British divisions.
BEF	British Expeditionary Force. Title of the British armies first sent to France in 1914. During the Third Ypres campaign the BEF was commanded by Field Marshal Haig.
Army (xxxx)	A headquarters, two or more corps and supporting units, containing 40,000 or more soldiers commanded by a general. General Plumer had three corps from the British Second Army for his initial Passchendaele attack.
Corps (xxx)	A headquarters with two or more divisions including additional units not in the division such as corps artillery or corps tank units. Comprises between 20,000 and 80,000 troops commanded by a lieutenant general such as Godley, who commanded II ANZAC Corps.
Division (xx)	A headquarters with three infantry brigades, supporting artillery, engineers, medical and logistic services, with 15,000 to 20,000 troops commanded by a major general. The division (such as the 3rd Australian Division commanded by Monash) comprised the basic unit of manoeuvre on the Western Front.
Brigade (x)	A headquarters, four infantry battalions, a machine-gun company and a trench mortar battery, around 3500 to 5000 troops commanded by a brigadier general. Brigade commanders in the 3rd Australian Division were Rosenthal (9th Brigade), McNicoll (10th Brigade) and Cannan (11th Brigade).
Battalion (II)	A headquarters, four rifle companies and support platoon, totalling 500 to 1000 troops commanded by a lieutenant colonel. A battalion is 'home' for the average soldier and the building block of the brigade.
Company (I)	A headquarters and four rifle platoons, some 100 to 200 troops, commanded by a major or captain.

Platoon 		A headquarters and three or four rifle sections of 30 to 50 troops commanded by a lieutenant.
Section 		Approximately 10 to 15 troops commanded by a corporal.

Allied Artillery Terms

Artillery Reserve	Artillery fire held back for use against unforeseen enemy targets.
Barrage	Artillery fire that is designed to cover an area held by the enemy rather than aimed at a specific point or target.
Box Barrage	Three or four barrages used to form a box around a position in order to isolate it, either for defensive or offensive purposes. At Messines box barrages were placed around Allied infantry holding captured German trench lines in order to deter German counter-attacks.
BGHA	Brigadier General Heavy Artillery
Creeping Barrage	Artillery fire placed in front of advancing troops. The fire would advance with the troops, typically at a rate of 100 metres every three minutes.
Counter-battery fire	Artillery fire used to destroy or neutralise enemy artillery.
FOO	Artillery Forward Observation Officer who directs artillery fire and usually moves with the advancing infantry.
Field (Light) Artillery	Artillery included within the division, used in a mobile role and engaging the enemy with direct fire. Later it would include howitzers, which could fire in the indirect role. Typically these were guns of between 7.6cm and 8.4cm calibre.
GOCRA	General Officer Commanding Royal Artillery — controlled artillery assets at corps level.
Heavy Artillery	Artillery used to attack fortifications, pillboxes and German artillery — typically a corps resource and between 156mm and 299mm calibre.
Predictive Fire	Artillery fire that dispenses with registration, ranging on a target by observation only. Predicted fire is placed on target through calculations based on trigonometry and incorporating a range of other variables such as weather.
Preliminary Bombardment	A barrage conducted to weaken and disrupt the enemy defence prior to an attack.
Medium Artillery	Artillery of more than 10.5cm calibre and up to 15.5cm calibre. Usually allocated to a division and used for counter-battery fire.

Allied Tactical Terms

Assault	The climax of an attack, usually involving hand-to-hand fighting.
Boundary	A demarcation or planning line between two units used to ensure they do not become intermingled in the heat of battle. Boundaries are often clear geographic features such as the Ypres–Zonnebeke railway line separating the 3rd and 4th Australian divisions.
Battlefield Clearance	A task undertaken forward of the main trench line after the battle has concluded. Typically soldiers undertaking battlefield clearance are looking for wounded, weapons, or items of enemy intelligence while also ensuring that no enemy reconnaissance elements remain close at hand.
Control Lines	Planning line drawn on maps and used by headquarters to control the progress of the battle such as the Red, Blue and Green lines of the 3rd Australian Division. Where possible, such lines are aligned with geographic features to make them obvious to advancing troops.
Counter-attack	An attack by the defending force against an enemy attacking force to regain lost ground or destroy the advancing enemy forces. A frequent German tactic was to use dedicated counter-attack divisions to recapture lost ground.
Defensive Line	A series of defended positions. In the early war years this was usually a linear trench position but later evolved to layers of individual defensive positions.
Enfilade Fire	Fire directed at a right angle against the flank of advancing troops such as the 10th Brigade experienced on its left flank from the German positions at Waterfields.
Frontage	The width of a unit when spread out for an attack. The width of the frontage will also determine its density. For example, Monash calculated a battalion frontage of 450 to 550 metres with a density of one soldier every metre during the Passchendaele attack.
Junction Point	Points on or near boundaries at which contact will be made with flanking units such as the junction point between I and II ANZAC Corps on the Ypres–Roulers railway line.
Mopping up	The liquidation of remnants of enemy resistance in an area through which other units have moved without eliminating all active resistance. For example, in the 10th Brigade plan, the 40th Battalion was tasked to mop up German elements that were not eliminated in the initial attack by other battalions.
Objective	The physical object/feature for which an attack is being conducted. The seizure of an objective, such as Passchendaele, is seen as essential to the success of a commander's plan.
Operational Level of War	The operational level of war is concerned with the planning and conduct of campaigns. It is at this level that national concepts of military strategy are decided by government and implemented by assigning armies and resources to specific campaigns such as Third Ypres.
Rate of Advance	The speed at which a military unit calculates it should advance in the face of enemy resistance, terrain and other relevant variables.

Reverse Slope	A slope on a hill that descends away from the enemy. A defence on a reverse slope provides protection from enemy observation and direct fire.
Reserves (army, corps, division, brigade, battalion, company, platoon)	Reserves are held by commanders at all levels of army organisation to deal with unforeseen circumstances. These circumstances may include repulsing enemy attacks or exploiting enemy weaknesses.
Salient	A salient is discrete territory projecting out of a main geographic position. This discrete territory is bordered by enemy-held ground on three sides. The Third Ypres campaign was based on Haig's decision to attack out of the Ypres salient.
Start Line	A line designated on a map and coordinated with a geographic feature which defines the departure point of an attack. Where a geographic feature is not available, other methods are used. On the evening of 11 October, the Brigade Majors of the 3rd Australian Division pegged out the various battalion start lines with stakes and tape.
Strategic Level of War	The level of war in which a nation or a group of nations determines national or multinational objectives and deploys military resources to achieve them. The decision by Britain and her dominions to deploy the BEF to the Western Front to assist France is one example.
Tactical Level of War	The tactical level of war is concerned with the planning and conduct of specific battles to achieve tactical objectives. Such battles are usually within a framework of operational objectives. Haig conducted a series of tactical battles — Messines, Pilckem Ridge, Menin Road, Polygon Wood, Poelcappelle and Passchendaele — in order to achieve his operational objective of securing the channel ports.
Trench Raid	A surprise attack on enemy positions often used to capture prisoners, gain intelligence and unsettle the opposing enemy. Can be conducted in any strength, from section to battalion.
German Defensive Terms	
Defence in Depth	A reaction to the superiority of Allied artillery, defence in depth replaced the linear trench line with a collection of layered fortified positions designed to absorb and then entrap an Allied attack. This enabled the German Army to hold the line with fewer men and also reduced the effectiveness of Allied artillery.
Outpost Line	The first of the three layers of a German battalion's defensive line, the outpost line provided early warning of an Allied attack. This line was thinly held by infantry scattered among shell holes.
Forward Zone	A zone containing one or two platoons and machine-guns from a company located some 500 metres forward of the Main Line of Resistance. To overcome the defences of the Forward Zone would require the Allies to commit substantial artillery resources to an attack, during which the Forward Zone troops would retreat to the Main Line of Resistance.
Main Line of Resistance	The area in which the bulk of a German battalion was located in company-sized positions with interconnecting trenches and wire to a depth of 300 to 400 metres. Equipped with machine-guns and infantry weapons, these troops hoped to absorb and then halt any Allied attack.

Local Defence Commander	The German battalion commander at the point of the Allied attack. This commander was also designated Commander of the Forward Troops and given control of all reinforcements fed into the defensive battle irrespective of the rank level of the reinforcing units. This was based on the principle that the commander on the spot was best suited to running the defensive battle. If the attack was too large for a battalion commander to manage, the divisional commander became the Local Defence Commander.

General Terms	
Brigade Major	The chief of staff in a brigade headquarters. The Brigade Major was also responsible for operational planning on the headquarters.
Doctrine	Principles by which military forces guide their actions, usually in support of higher objectives.
'Over the top'	To leave the safety of a defensive position and advance into battle.
Pillbox	A general BEF term for any German fortified structure.
War Diary	The official journal of a unit describing its daily war activities. Usually written by an officer such as the Adjutant, war diaries vary considerably in both length and detail depending on the enthusiasm and time availability of the author.
Organisational Tables	A list of manpower and equipment that was authorised to make up a unit. The AIF was primarily raised and equipped according to British Army organisational tables.

INTRODUCTION

More than any of the conflicts in which Australians have fought, the battles of the First World War must be placed in context if the efforts of Australian soldiers are to be understood. War on the Western Front was the domain of army groups, armies and corps, where the division was the basic building block for the corps and the corps the basis for the planning of any battle. This is significantly different to Australian military organisation in the Second World War where the battalion and the brigade were often the foundations of military planning, particularly for the battles of the south-west Pacific. The sheer scale of action on the Western Front means that any decision to focus on a single division risks losing the context of the broader picture, without which the actions of that single division cannot be fairly evaluated. This is particularly true of the divisions of the Australian Imperial Force (AIF) in 1917. They and other dominion troops comprised a minority force operating alongside the British Army under the command structure of the British Expeditionary Force (BEF). The BEF was, in turn, a junior partner to the French Army, which provided the bulk of the Allied forces on the Western Front.

The actions of the 3rd Australian Division at Passchendaele have to be viewed within this framework. It did not conduct independent operations, but fought within a corps structure using British equipment and doctrine. In doing so, the division achieved a level of integration with the British Army which would be the envy of any present-day coalition operation. Such close integration brought considerable benefits to the AIF and enabled it to realise a level of military proficiency that would have taken much longer to attain—if it attained such a level at all—had it been left to its own resources. However it also meant that Australia's political and military leadership willingly acquiesced to British war aims, methods and campaigns.

Battles are usually the result of broader strategic and operational design. To understand why the battle for Passchendaele was fought, the campaign of which it was a component also requires study. As the name implies, the Third Battle of Ypres was not the first time this town in western Flanders had been a focus of interest. The town lay north-east of the great sweep of the German armies through neutral Belgium in August-September 1914 and only came to prominence as the German and Allied armies attempted to outflank one another during their rush to the channel coast in October-November 1914. Over this period, referred to as the First Battle of Ypres, Allied forces managed to establish a continuous front and repel German attempts to capture the town. Stiff Allied resistance at Ypres saw the town become a salient, protruding into the German line. The Second Battle of Ypres was fought between April and May 1915 and was the result of a German attempt to eliminate the salient. The outcome of the battles forced the Allied lines closer to Ypres, and saw Germans take control of the ridges around the town.

The Allied offensive conducted between June and November 1917 to break out of the Ypres salient and capture the Belgian channel ports was known as the Third Battle of Ypres. The preparation and conduct of this offensive dominated the activities of the BEF for the latter half of 1917. Over this period a number of individual battles were fought. These began with feint attacks by Allied forces towards Lens and Lille (26—30 June 1917), moved to a preliminary operation at the Battle of Messines (7—14 June 1917), and finally settled into a sequence of battles: the Battle of Pilckem Ridge (31 July—2 August 1917), the Battle of Langemarck (16—18 August), the Battle of Menin Road (20—25

September 1917), the Battle of Polygon Wood (26 September 1917), the Battle of Broodseinde (4 October 1917) and the Battle of Poelcappelle (9 October 1917). This Allied offensive culminated in the two battles for Passchendaele, beginning with the attack by II ANZAC Corps on 12 October 1917 and followed by the attacks of the Canadian Corps from 26 October to 10 November 1917.

Post-war criticism of the architect of the Third Ypres campaign, Field Marshal Sir Douglas Haig, has tended to focus on two issues associated with Passchendaele: first, the accusation that the operational circumstances did not justify fighting the battle, and second, given the ground conditions, that the attacking Allied troops did not have a reasonable chance of success. To address these issues requires not only an examination of Passchendaele within the context of the campaign, but an understanding of the nature of battle in 1917. For both sides of the line, the battle for Passchendaele represented the apex of a broader pyramid, the foundations of which were training, organisation, doctrine and technology. Thus, a study of the way Australian divisional structure, tactics and weaponry had evolved prior to Passchendaele, together with a similar description of the evolution of the German forces charged with its defence, will set the scene for a more nuanced understanding of how the 3rd Australian Division conducted its attack. Since nothing illuminates failure like success, a brief description of the successful Canadian attacks on Passchendaele is also included, allowing a direct comparison with the Australian approach.

Finally, it is worth discussing some of the terminology associated with the battle for Passchendaele. This battle occurred in two parts, the first an unsuccessful attempt by the Australian 3rd Division to capture the village on 12 October 1917, and the second the successful Canadian attacks from 26 October to 10 November 1917. There are differences between the British *Official History of the War* and the Australian *Official History* when it comes to the labelling of these two battles. The British *Official History* describes the Australian 12 October 1917 assault on Passchendaele as the First Battle of Passchendaele (Passchendaele I) and the Canadian attacks from 26 October to 10 November 1917 as the Second Battle of Passchendaele (Passchendaele II). In contrast, the Australian *Official History* by C.E.W Bean names the 9 October 1917 attack on Poelcappelle as Passchendaele I and the Australian 12 October 1917 assault on Passchendaele as Passchendaele II. The subsequent Canadian attacks are also considered part of Passchendaele II.

There is some logic in Bean's labelling, since the 9 October 1917 attack was viewed in the Australian *Official History* as a 'short preparatory advance' for the subsequent attack on Passchendaele. The British *Official History* labels Poelcappelle as an attack to 'reach more than half way [sic] towards the day's objective' (Passchendaele) which would then offer an opportunity to pursue the Germans well beyond the village and the associated ridge. While the distinction between the two definitions is so fine as to be meaningless, this study will use the terminology of the British *Official History* and call the Australian attack on 12 October 1917 the First Battle of Passchendaele (Passchendaele I), if for no other reason than this particular label has more common usage and makes a clear distinction between this and the subsequent Canadian attacks at the Second Battle of Passchendaele (Passchendaele II).

1

CHAPTER I

PASSCHENDAELE: THE OPERATIONAL BACKGROUND TO THE BATTLE

GENESIS OF THE THIRD YPRES OFFENSIVE

An aerial view of Ypres taken from an Allied observation balloon on 31 October 1917. The Cloth Hall and Ypres Cathedral are at the top left of the picture (AWM E01257).

In 1917 Ypres had been transformed from what had previously been a prosperous market town in the Flemish part of Belgium to one of the most important locations on the Western Front. Not only had two major campaigns been fought for its possession in 1914 and 1915, but in 1917 it formed the base of a salient into the German lines, providing a potential starting point for any Allied offensive towards the Belgian ports. The town itself lay on the Yser Canal and derived its military significance from being a road, rail and canal junction linking northern France and Belgium. However, the cost to the town of this significance was high. A British Army padre visiting Ypres in September 1917 described a large a town that had been reduced to ruins, with not a single habitable dwelling. The dominant pre-war feature of the town was the Cloth Hall, one of the Middle Age's largest commercial structures, but bombardment had reduced this unique building to a bare shell. In 1917 the damaged tower of the Cloth Hall was still standing, and was one of the few vertical landmarks in an otherwise horizontal landscape of stone and rubble.

The geography of the region around Ypres is dominated by flat, agricultural plains, broken only by a series of low ridges which form a semi-circle around the south, east and north-east side of the town. South-east of Ypres are the villages of Wytschaete and Messines, which sit on the southern end of the Ypres Ridge. Almost 4 kilometres due north of Ypres is a small feature named Pilckem Ridge which runs in between, and parallel with, the Yser Canal and Steenbeek Creek. All of these features run in a north-south direction. Any advance east of these obstacles would encounter slowly rising ground until it reached the northern end of the Ypres Ridge.

Contemporary farmhouses on the main road (Passendalestraat) leading into Passchendaele village. This gives an impression of what the housing and terrain would have looked like prior to the war (image courtesy of Bill Fraser).

The central mass of the Ypres Ridge was the Gheluvelt Plateau, a flat area crossed by the Ypres—Menin road. Moving north from the

Gheluvelt Plateau the ridge narrowed, but provided sufficient level ground to support the villages of Passchendaele, Westroosebeke and Staden. These villages had provided housing for local businessmen and landowners and the houses were generally of a more substantial nature than those associated with the farming communities on the plains, although by 1917 these villages were in ruins. Small woods and coppice had dotted the Ypres Ridge, but these forested areas were now destroyed. The resulting debris of stumps and broken tree limbs fused with the churned soil, presenting a significant obstacle to advancing infantry or tanks.

The Ypres battlefield south-east of Broodseinde on 28 September 1917. To the right the ground starts to rise towards the ridge line which would lead to Passchendaele (AWM E00893).

The military significance of the Ypres Ridge lay in the flatness of the surrounding plain. Despite an average height of just 40 to 50 metres (around 60 metres at its highest points), possession of the ridge provided German forces with clear observation of Allied activity in Ypres and the surrounding area, while also obscuring Allied observation of German movements behind the ridge. Because of this, no Allied offensive could move north to the Belgian coast without first securing its left flank on the Ypres Ridge.

A British plan to recapture the Belgian ports of Ostend, Blankenberghe and Zeebrugge from the Germans was first proposed in December 1914 by Winston Churchill, then First Lord of the Admiralty, to the commander of the BEF, Sir John French. Given their location, flanking the main cross-channel troop and supply routes from the British ports of Richborough, Dover and Folkestone to the French ports of Dunkirk, Calais and Boulogne, the Admiralty's interest in recapturing the Belgian ports was self-evident. Their ownership gave German naval forces harbours from which to interdict the vital Allied channel supply links while also supporting German U-boat operations in the Atlantic. In November 1915 the Admiralty presented another proposal to capture the ports to the new commander of the BEF, Field Marshal Sir Douglas Haig. The

Admiralty plan involved an amphibious landing near Ostend supported by a limited land offensive from Nieuport. Haig, while supportive of the concept, considered the frontage of the proposed land operation too narrow, confined as it was between coastal dunes and the inland marshes of the Yser River. His concept was far bolder, involving a major offensive from the Ypres salient sweeping north-west to capture Bruges and the entire coastline between Nieuport and Zeebrugge.

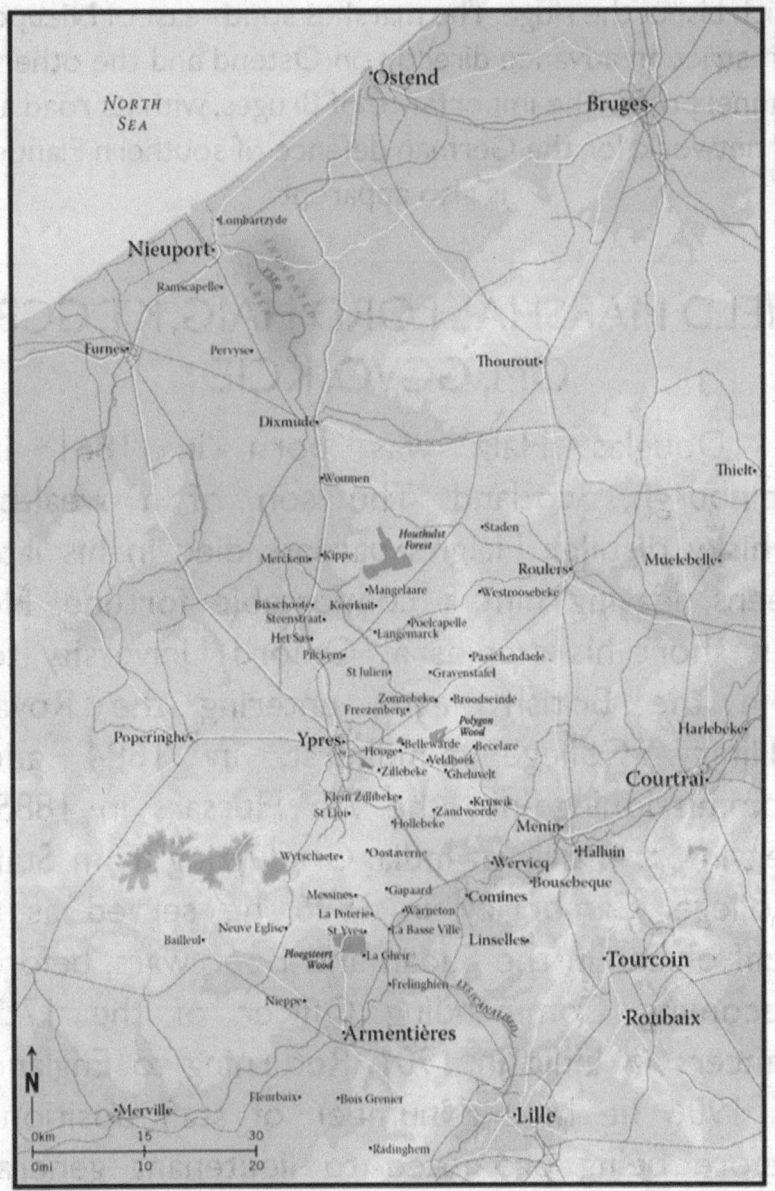

Map 1. The topography of the Ypres area in 1917 showing its significance as a road, rail and canal communications hub. The dominant geographic feature is the crescent-shaped ridge line beginning south of Ypres and sweeping north-east to Passchendaele. The Ypres to Roulers railway line and the Ypres to Menin road are the two transport corridors

which bisect the ridge. The marshes south-east of Nieuport restrict an advance directly on Ostend and the other channel ports. The importance of Bruges, with its road and rail network, for the German defence of southern Flanders is also apparent.

FIELD MARSHAL LORD HAIG, KT, GCB, OM, GCVO, KCIE

Douglas Haig was born in 1861 in Edinburgh, Scotland. The son of a wealthy whisky distiller, Haigh's parents died in his late teens, leaving him a comfortable fortune. He cut short his studies at Oxford University to join the British Army, entering the Royal Military College, Sandhurst, in 1884 and commissioning into the 7th Hussars in 1885, serving primarily in India. Graduating from Staff College, Camberley, in 1896, he served as a staff officer in the Sudan and Boer wars, before becoming Commanding Officer of the 17th Lancers in India in 1901. Returning to England in 1906 he held a number of staff positions before being promoted to lieutenant general and assuming the position of Chief of the General Staff for the Indian Army in 1909, laying the ground work for the Indian Expeditionary Force. Haig left India in 1912 to become General Officer Commanding (GOC) Aldershot Command. At the outbreak of war in 1914, Aldershot Command became I Corps, giving Haig command of one of the two BEF corps. Haig's I Corps played a critical role in blunting the German attack during the First Battle of Ypres in October and November 1914 and he took command of the newly formed First Army in December 1914. Following the British setbacks in 1915, Haig replaced Sir John French as Commander-in-Chief of the BEF in December 1915. At the time of his appointment Haig was 54 years old and had achieved the most important field appointment in the British Army. He would lead the BEF through the battles of the Somme, Arras, Third Ypres, the German Spring Offensive and the Hundred Days. After the war Haig served as Commander-in-Chief Home Forces before retiring from the Army in January 1920. He devoted the remainder of his life to the welfare of ex-servicemen and died of a heart attack aged 66 in 1928. He was buried at Dryburg Abbey in the Scottish borders, his grave marked by the standard Commonwealth War Graves Commission headstone.

Haig as Commander-in-Chief of the BEF (AWM A03713).

Haig had fought as a corps commander in the First Battle of Ypres, so he was well acquainted with the ground around Ypres.

Admiralty priorities, combined with his familiarity with the ground, may have had a bearing on what appeared to be his longstanding preference for a Flanders-based offensive. On 14 January 1916 he instructed the commander of the British Second Army, General Sir Hubert Plumer, to consider plans for a major offensive launched from Ypres. On 4 February Haig further directed Lieutenant General Sir Henry Rawlinson, who was due to take command of Fourth Army, to also consider the option. Three weeks later, on 27 February, Rawlinson submitted to Haig his six-stage plan for an offensive from Ypres, the first stage of which included capturing the Messines Ridge, south-east of Ypres. Marshal Joseph Joffre, as Commander-in-Chief of the French Army, also gave approval for a Flanders-based offensive as the main British effort for 1916. However, the German attack at Verdun in late February almost immediately disrupted Allied consideration of a Flanders offensive. Heavy French losses resulted in the commitment of the British Fourth Army to the Somme in an attempt to draw German reserves away from Verdun. The Verdun offensive also dictated that Allied strategy in 1916 would be primarily defensive, its main objective to relieve the increasing pressure on the French Army. Any major Allied offensive in Flanders in 1916 was now unlikely.

Despite this setback, Haig ordered the commander of the newly formed Reserve Army, General Sir Hubert Gough, to begin planning stage one (the capture of the Messines Ridge) of the Rawlinson Ypres offensive plan.

Determined to regain the strategic initiative in 1917, Joffre called a conference on 15 November 1916 to discuss Allied plans for the coming year. The conference emphasised the primacy of the Western Front over other theatres of war. It also agreed to a British and French offensive in the Somme and Aisne sectors, with the main Allied effort then switching to Flanders. It was anticipated that this series of battles would sufficiently degrade German reserves to enable a decisive Allied offensive in Flanders by late 1917. Following the conference, Haig again asked Plumer to submit a plan for a Flanders offensive, which he duly did on 12 December 1916. Allied unanimity to proceed with a Flanders offensive lasted barely three weeks as, in early December, Joffre was replaced by Robert Nivelle as Commander-in-Chief of the French Army. Nivelle wanted the French Army to undertake a major offensive in 1917 in the Soissons-Reims area with the British Army to play a subsidiary role at Arras. Haig agreed to the Nivelle plan, reasoning that, if the French offensive succeeded, German reserves would be withdrawn from the Flanders area, increasing the chances of success for any possible Ypres offensive.

On 6 January 1917 Haig asked Plumer to recast his Ypres offensive plan in light of Nivelle's new strategic priorities. Plumer presented his revised plan to Haig on 30 January. In broad terms, Plumer's initial operation employed a northern army (Fourth Army) to capture Pilckem Ridge and, on the same day, a southern army (Second Army) to capture Messines and advance across part of the Gheluvelt Plateau. Once the southern army had achieved its objectives, the northern army could advance on Passchendaele and position itself for a subsequent breakout to the channel coast. In essence, the success of the southern army would provide a secure right flank for the advance of the northern army, with the left flank of the northern army covered by Belgian divisions attacking from Clercken-Zarren. These moves would be complemented by either French or British forces attacking along the coast at Nieuport to link up with a British amphibious landing near Ostend.

Haig considered proposed changes to Plumer's plan from both General Rawlinson and a planning team from his own headquarters staff (headed by Lieutenant Colonel Macmullen from his Operations Branch). In reviewing Plumer's plan, Rawlinson's primary misgiving concerned the northern army and what would happen to its attack on Pilckem Ridge should the southern army fail to capture Messines or the Gheluvelt Plateau. He also argued that the attacks could not take place simultaneously. Both the northern and southern armies required the same piece of ground from which to launch their operations and Rawlinson considered there was insufficient room to accommodate the artillery required for simultaneous attacks. Macmullen also recognised the limitations of space, but proposed to attack all three objectives (Pilckem Ridge, the Gheluvelt Plateau and Messines) simultaneously, using artillery to target Pilckem Ridge and Messines only, and utilising tanks to capture the Gheluvelt Plateau. Haig initially supported this Macmullen variation to Plumer's plan, but a reconnaissance of the ground in April by a tank officer revealed that the intended sector was unsuitable for the employment of tanks. This information, combined with the shortage of tanks, saw the Macmullen tank variation dropped. During these discussions Haig accepted Rawlinson's concerns over the Gheluvelt Plateau and the potential for crowding associated with launching simultaneous attacks. Plumer's plan was modified to an initial attack on Messines and the western edge of the Gheluvelt Plateau, followed by a subsequent attack on Pilckem Ridge—but without specifying the time interval between the two attacks.

While Haig was satisfied with the fundamentals of Plumer's plan, he was less enthusiastic over proposals for the way the battles would be conducted. Both Plumer and Rawlinson envisaged a series of limited advances, based on infantry assaults heavily supported by artillery which would seize objectives in the German front line. The infantry would then hold this ground against the inevitable German counter-attacks, with the support of the same artillery which had assisted the limited attack. The key to this tactic was for the infantry not to move outside the protective umbrella provided by Allied artillery fire. When compared to a general offensive these tactics, named 'bite and hold', limited Allied exposure to casualties while depleting any German reserves that should counter-attack. The disadvantage of the 'bite and hold' tactics, however, was that no single battle could achieve a significant breakout. Success in limited attacks would only result from the attrition of German forces.

This was clearly not Haig's intent for any Ypres offensive. His vision included a breakout from the German defensive lines, followed by an advance north to the channel ports. In this plan Haig reflected the motivations of both the French and British governments in 1916 which sought a 1917 strategy that could possibly conclude the war, rather than one more likely to prolong the strategic status quo by defeating Germany through attrition. Within this context it is hardly surprising that Haig sought an officer with a similar view to his own on the conduct of the operation. Haig's selection of General Hubert Gough as commander for the northern army may well have been based on his relationship with Brigadier General 'Johnnie' Gough, Hubert Gough's brother, who had served as Haig's Chief of Staff when he was commander of I Army Corps.

The failure of the Nivelle offensive (despite the British success at Arras) in April-May 1917 also meant another recasting of the Ypres offensive. A Franco-British military conference was held on the morning of 4 May, followed by an inter-Allied conference in the afternoon, to discuss possible Allied options for the remainder of 1917. At this stage, unknown to the British, the French position at the two conferences was increasingly influenced by developments within the French Army. The defeat of the Nivelle offensive, following so closely after heavy losses at Verdun, was generating a crisis of confidence within the Army and, in late April, the first mutinies occurred, the majority taking place between 25 May and 10 June 1917. As events were to illustrate, while these mutinies had only a limited impact on the defensive capabilities of the French Army, they significantly reduced its ability to undertake offensive action. While not immediately dismissed after his failed offensive, Nivelle was in the process of being moved to one side, with General Philippe Pétain becoming Chief of the General Staff on 29 April and then commander of the French armies in north and north-east France from 17 May 1917.

Both conferences concluded that a decisive breakthrough of the German lines was now unlikely and that the best the Allies could hope for in 1917 was to maintain pressure on the German Army through a series of attacks with limited objectives. It was believed that such a strategy would deplete the reserves of German manpower and prevent their recovery from losses incurred in the April-May offensive. Given the exhaustion of the French Army, it was also agreed that the British Army would carry the main burden of any future offensive operations, with the French Army playing a supporting role. The French Premier, Alexandre Ribot, and the British Prime Minister, David Lloyd George, agreed that any further military planning would not aim to achieve operational breakthroughs, but rather concentrate on wearing down German resistance as a means of creating strategic opportunities. This approach reflected both the limitations of the French Army and the increasing possibility that German successes on the Eastern Front would enable them to transfer significant numbers of divisions to the west. If this was the case, the Allies would have to survive a possible German offensive in late 1917 or early 1918 before American reinforcements would arrive on the Western Front in significant numbers.

Haig noted in his diary after discussions with Pétain at the Franco-British military conference on 4 May 1917 that the plans for any 1917 offensive would be kept secret from both governments. They were prepared to reveal the principles of any offensive, but not the specifics. Haig did not elaborate on why this was agreed, but presumably it was an attempt to preserve security. Later that day, at the inter-Allied conference, Lloyd George stated that the time, method and place of any offensives would be left to the Allied military leadership. This obviously pleased Haig, who now felt he had the approval of the Prime Minister to conduct an offensive in the manner of his choosing. However, in his *War Memoirs*, Lloyd George provides an interpretation of the conference outcomes which was diametrically opposed to that of Haig. Lloyd George cites Haig's assertion that any future offensives on the Western Front would be limited, designed only to attrite German forces while preserving Allied strength. Lloyd George believed that this ruled out any large-scale BEF offensive to breach the German line in Flanders and clear the Belgian coast—the very offensive that Haig was now planning and for which he believed he had the full support of his Prime Minister.

Haig assembled his commanders on 7 May 1917 to discuss the outcome of the conferences. He restated the conference strategy of conducting limited battles of attrition, revealing also that the British Army would conduct the major offensive in 1917 at Ypres. Clearly Haig did not see any contradiction in these two positions, with limited battles of attrition viewed merely as a tactic within his larger offensive strategy. Following the Arras battles there would be a gradual transfer of resources to the north. The fundamentals of the 30 January 1917 offensive plan also remained unchanged. Messines, Pilckem Ridge and the Gheluvelt Plateau would be secured, followed by a drive from Passchendaele to capture the channel ports. The first phase of the offensive would involve an attack on Messines Ridge on 7 June followed by a second phase a few weeks later, with attacks on Pilckem Ridge and the Gheluvelt Plateau. This was a crucial change, since the delay between the attack on Messines and the subsequent attacks on Pilckem Ridge and the Gheluvelt Plateau solved the problem of the lack of space and artillery resources to conduct simultaneous attacks from the same piece of ground. While this decision resolved critical time and space issues for Haig, it was done so at the cost of operational surprise. Once the Messines attack commenced, it would provide the German High Command a significant indicator of possible future Allied intentions in Flanders. This, combined with an eventual gap of seven weeks between the Messines battle and the next phase of the offensive, also afforded the Germans an opportunity to redeploy and reinforce their defences.

Haig hoped that any adverse effects resulting from the delay between the two phases of the operation would be covered by Allied feints that would persuade the Germans that Messines was a discrete operation rather than a preliminary attack to a larger Ypres offensive. In a meeting with Haig on 18 May 1917, Pétain described preparations for four attacks between June and July which could be synchronised with the Ypres offensive. While objecting to the Ypres offensive as contradicting the 4 May 1917 inter-Allied conference philosophy of limited attacks, Pétain recognised the political imperative for the Allies to move to the offensive. Haig argued that his series of attacks would be conducted with limited objectives which, through a process of attrition, would produce opportunities for advances over much greater distances. French promises of support eventually materialised, but not in the promised time frames due to the disciplinary problems within the French Army.

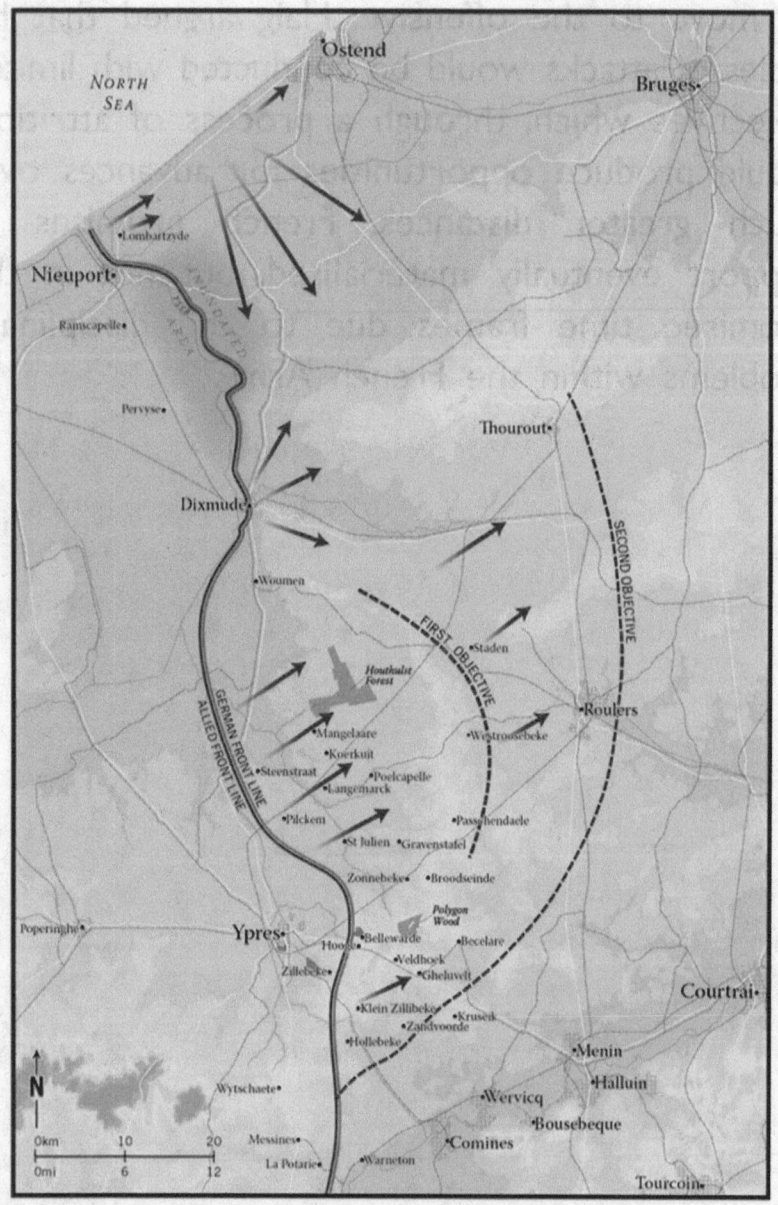

Map 2. The outline of Haig's plan for the Flanders campaign as provided to General Pétain on 18 May 1917. Limited attacks from Nieuport and Dixmude include an amphibious landing south-west of Ostend. The campaign is to be conducted in two phases with the first objective a line from Passchendaele to Staden and the second objective Roulers

to Thourout. The Allied start line appears to assume the success of the Messines attack in June 1917.

Against the backdrop of the uncertain nature of French support and the deteriorating fortunes of Allied forces on the Russian and Italian fronts, Haig's proposed Ypres offensive was considered by the British Cabinet Committee on War Policy in a series of meetings in late June 1917. Lloyd George, while supporting offensive action, was sceptical of the scale of the proposed offensive and preferred the limited attacks as recommended by the 4 May conference. Haig argued that Lloyd George did not give sufficient weight to the German losses inflicted by the Somme offensive, adding that, should the British Army not conduct the Ypres offensive, this would represent a missed opportunity. While Lloyd George preferred to divert British divisions to the Italian front, the primacy of conducting an operation on the Western Front was agreed. The First Sea Lord, Admiral Jellicoe, restated the Admiralty's position on the importance of recapturing the channel ports. Without this, Jellicoe maintained that Britain would be unable to continue the war into 1918 given the heavy losses to British shipping inflicted by German U-boats. In the face of recommendations by both Haig and Jellicoe on 20 July 1917 the committee reluctantly agreed to the Ypres offensive—some 36 days after the Messines preliminary operation had been completed (7—14 June 1917) and just 11 days before the launching of the actual offensive on 31 July 1917. Given the considerable planning and organisation required to conduct a major offensive, it is clear that this activity was already well under way prior to the meeting of the Cabinet Committee on War Policy.

Haig's intent for the forthcoming offensive was outlined at a commanders' conference on 7 May, followed by written orders from his headquarters on 22 May. The main offensive by Gough's Fifth Army (the northern army) would be conducted with 18 divisions, with Plumer's Second Army (the southern army) allocated 12 divisions. Second Army had three corps, including II ANZAC Corps, with I ANZAC Corps added in late July as a reserve. The key players in the 12 October Passchendaele attack, the 3rd Australian Division and the New Zealand Division, were both part of II ANZAC Corps.

More than half of the artillery from Second Army was transferred to Fifth Army following Messines. The remaining guns in Second Army (243 heavy howitzers and 546 field guns) were concentrated on the Second/Fifth Army boundary in support of Fifth Army's northern operations. Other British artillery resources on the Western

Front were also transferred to Fifth Army which, over a three-week period, enjoyed an increase in heavy howitzers and field guns from 203 and 444 to 752 and 1422 respectively. This heavy concentration of artillery in Fifth Army underlines the emphasis of the Haig plan on its proposed breakout to the channel ports. Other resources allocated to the offensive included 406 aircraft and 18 kite balloon sections. Three tank brigades (216 tanks) were also attached to Fifth Army. Some 64 labour companies were moved to Ypres, including two Canadian and three West Indies battalions and 28 companies of the Labour Corps. Among these were Chinese labour companies and, by October 1917, some 50,000 Chinese were employed in labour companies on the Ypres front. As the Ypres offensive developed and the weather deteriorated, the role and capabilities of the labour companies in maintaining the lines of communication would become crucial for the future momentum of the offensive.

MESSINES—THE PRELIMINARY OPERATION

The opening moves of the Third Battle of Ypres saw feint attacks conducted south of the Ypres salient over the period 26—30 June 1917 as part of Haig's deception plan. Feint attacks, by definition, are not the key point of any attack, but are designed to mask or distract enemy forces from the main effort. To be successful, feint attacks usually required the commitment of sufficient forces to raise doubts in the mind of an opposing commander over the true location of any future offensive. Haig's feint attacks were conducted by the British First Army towards Lens and the British Second Army towards Lille. The latter included the 3rd Australian Division, which launched local attacks near Douve designed to capture German picket lines and outposts. Effective German resistance to these feints made it obvious that any significant progress would require the commitment of larger forces—but this was not in accordance with Haig's plan. Given their limited success, it is doubtful whether the feints proved effective in distracting German attention from the Ypres salient.

Three corps of the British Second Army were employed in the Messines attack. The II ANZAC Corps objective was the village of Messines and the southern shoulder of the Messines Ridge, while IX Corps would attack the centre of the Messines Ridge and take the village of Wytschaete. The X Corps objective was the northern part of the ridge. Each corps would deploy three divisions in the assault and one division as a reserve. Seventy-four Mark IV tanks were also employed, their task to deal with German strongpoints and machine-guns.

In total, 2266 artillery pieces were assembled for the attack, organised into bombardment and counter-bombardment groups, which were then allocated to each corps. The artillery fire plan was based on experience gained from Arras and Vimy a few months earlier. It was designed to defeat the German defensive tactic of only lightly holding the front-line trenches, with a network of pillboxes and strongpoints arrayed immediately behind to ensnare any attacking infantry. Once weakened, the attacking infantry would be subjected to strong German counter-attacks. To counter this defensive doctrine, the British artillery bombarded the front-line positions as well as those strongpoints that constituted the German depth positions. At the same time, German artillery was subjected to a counter-battery campaign designed to weaken its ability to conduct defensive and offensive fire (some 3.5 million artillery shells were expended between 26 May and 6 June to achieve these aims). Following the launch of the attack, the German counter-attacks would be broken up by creeping barrages placed in front of the advancing infantry or in box barrages once the infantry were holding parts of the German line.

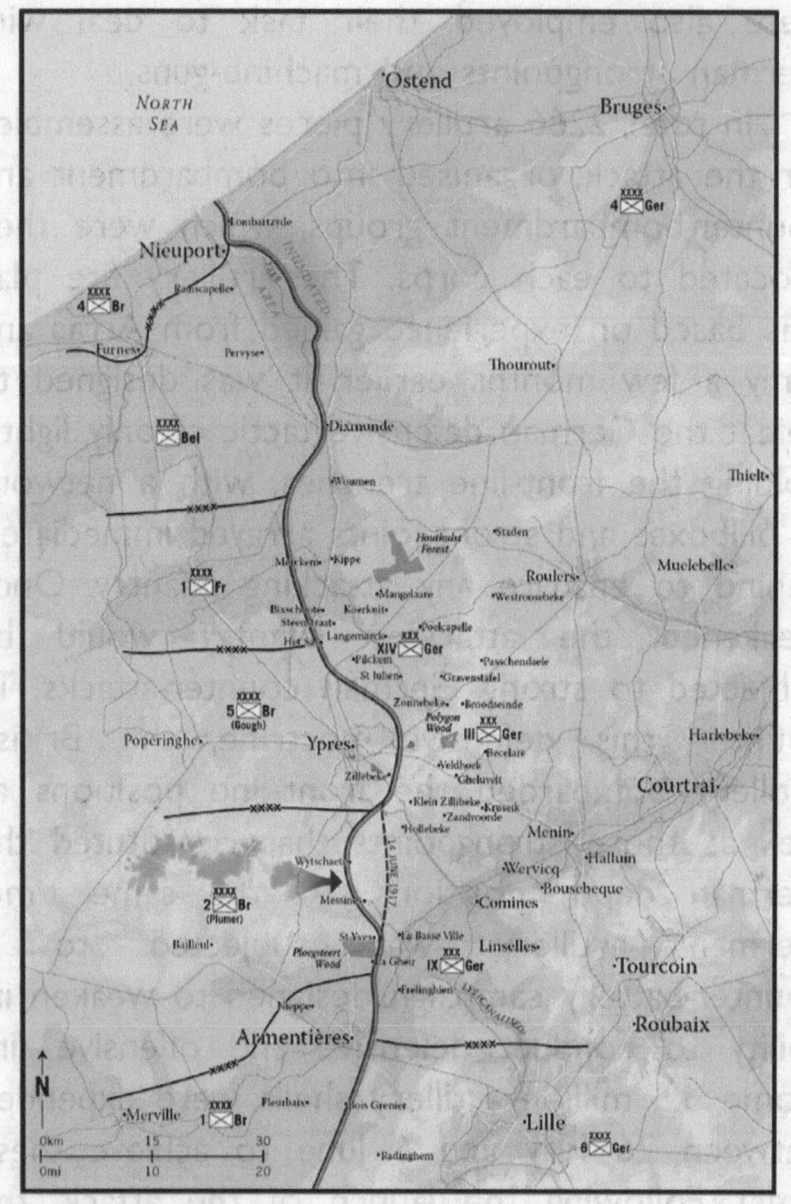

Map 3. The Allied gains at the Battle of Messines, 7-14 June 1917.

GENERAL SIR HUBERT DE LA POER GOUGH, GCB, GCMG, KCVO

Born in London in 1870, Hubert de la Poer Gough was the product of an Anglo-Irish family who had won three Victoria Crosses. His father was General Sir Charles Gough and, as a boy, Hubert Gough spent extended periods apart from his mother and father due to his father's service in India and Afghanistan. Gough entered the Royal Military Academy, Sandhurst, in 1888 and was commissioned into the 16th (The Queen's) Lancers in 1889. He served on the North West Frontier from 1897 to 1898 before entering Staff College, Camberley, in 1899, but did not complete the course due to service in the Boer War. Returning to Great Britain, he became an instructor at Staff College from 1904 to 1906 and was appointed Commanding Officer of the 16th (The Queen's) Lancers in 1907. In 1911 he was given the temporary rank of brigadier general and appointed GOC 3rd Cavalry Brigade. Gough's career was almost destroyed by the 'Curragh Mutiny' in March 1914 during which he emerged as one of the champions of the Ulster cause within the British Army. At the outbreak of war Gough took the 3rd Cavalry Brigade to France and was soon promoted to GOC 2nd Cavalry Division. He became commander of the 7th Division in April

1915, I Corps in July 1915 and GOC Reserve Corps in April 1916. In May 1916 Gough became an Army commander as his Reserve Corps was renamed the Reserve Army. Gough's rapid rise owed much to Haig's patronage. Haig admired Gough for his professionalism and aggression, but this did not prevent him shifting the main effort of the Third Ypres offensive away from Gough following the failure of his attack on 31 July 1917. After Third Ypres, Gough's Fifth Army bore the brunt of the German 1918 Spring Offensive and Gough was made the scapegoat for what were perceived as Fifth Army deficiencies. He handed over command of Fifth Army in March 1918. After the war Gough was appointed Chief of the Allied Military Mission to the Baltic in 1919, before retiring from the Army in 1922. During the interwar period Gough engaged in a number of farming and business ventures and, with the outbreak of the Second World War, joined the Home Guard. Much of his post-war years were spent rehabilitating his reputation following his 1918 dismissal. He died in London in 1963, aged 92.

General Gough (right) and King Albert I of Belgium at the entrance to a captured German dugout at Ginchy, France, 16 May 1917 (AWM H12215).

A feature of the Messines attack was the employment of mines placed under the German front lines. The use of mines was the mainstay of a plan conceived as far back as September 1915, with large-scale construction of tunnels and galleries commencing in January 1917. Extensive galleries were pushed towards the German front line from a start point 270 to 360 metres behind the British front line. Once beneath the German positions, chambers were dug and then packed with explosives. In total, 24 mines were placed, with 19 blown on the morning of 7 June, just prior to the infantry assault. The shock of the mine blasts stunned or killed the German troops, blowing large gaps in their defence which the Allied infantry subsequently occupied. The most significant impediment to the Allied advance came not from German defensive fire, but from the size of the craters produced by the mines.

The Messines attack proved enormously successful, with all initial objectives achieved. Each corps then established a front line on the eastern slope of its newly captured positions, with the main line of resistance on the top of the ridge, while the anticipated German counter-attacks were broken up by artillery. By clearing the Messines Ridge of German troops and gaining a foothold on the western end of the Gheluvelt Plateau, the necessary preconditions had been established for the main Ypres offensive to the north-east. At an army commanders' conference on 14 June, Haig reiterated that his objectives for the Ypres offensive had not changed from those outlined in the 7 May conference. While publicly confident of the likelihood of success, privately Haig was more circumspect. His diary entry of 14 June lists capture of the villages of Passchendaele and Staden on the northern arm of the Ypres Ridge and Clercken, north-east of Pilckem Ridge, as the initial objectives for the post-Messines attacks. Haig noted that, if these villages could not be captured without heavy losses in troops and artillery, then the other two objectives of the Ypres offensive (the push towards Roulers-Thourout and the amphibious assault/attack from Nieuport) might have to be cancelled.

GENERAL GOUGH AND FIFTH ARMY

With the Messines—Wytschaete ridge now secure, the focus shifted from Plumer and Second Army to General Gough and his Fifth Army. Gough had five corps at his disposal: the British II, XIV, XVIII and XIX Corps with V Corps in reserve. At a meeting of his corps commanders on 6—7 June, Gough outlined the basis of his plan. Put simply, this was to pivot on his left flank, while his right flank advanced up Passchendaele Ridge. The Fifth Army advance would be supported by the French First Army on its left, which would provide the hinge for the pivot, with the British Second Army on his right. Because Gough did not want Fifth Army to advance through the Houthulst Forest, he sought an active role for the French First Army in the attack. II ANZAC Corps from Plumer's Second Army would also participate in the attack, its progress dependent on Fifth Army's rate of advance. Gough also extended the Fifth/Second Army boundary south by some 1100 metres to include more of the Ypres Ridge within his area of operations.

At a commanders' conference on 14 June Haig gave the approximate date for the Fifth Army offensive as 25 July. At the insistence of the commander of the French First Army, who wanted more time for counter-battery fire, Haig moved the start date to 31 July. While the delay of six weeks between the conclusion of the Messines battle and the commencement of the Fifth Army attack would cost Haig operational surprise, given the time required to shift guns and material from Second Army to Fifth Army, this was unavoidable. Haig also had concerns over the impact of the weather on the offensive. His Intelligence Section, in a search of the Flanders meteorological records, discovered that October was the wettest month, although the period of wet weather normally began in August. However, pressed by his subordinate commanders for more time to complete their preparations, Haig accepted the risk and agreed to postpone the start date until 31 July. Gough was to write in his post-war memoirs that the delay of the offensive from the 25 July until 31 July would prove fatal, since on 31 July the weather broke and heavy rain turned the ground to a quagmire.

However, any apprehension Gough may have harboured over the weather appears to have been retrospective, since his own preparations were not completed until 28 July and the British *Official History* states that he was quite happy to wait the extra three days requested by the French.

Gough's planned attack on 31 July would occur in four stages. Stage one involved an advance of some 900 metres which would capture the first German defensive line between the Gheluvelt Plateau and Pilckem Ridge. There would be a 30-minute pause before stage two commenced, which comprised another advance of 900 metres to capture the second German defensive line on the reverse slope of Pilckem Ridge. After a pause of four hours, stage three would see a 1400-metre advance over the Steenbeek River to the village of St Julien and the third German defensive line. All told, these three stages represented an advance to a depth of 3.2 kilometres over a frontage of 12.8 kilometres. Having reached this point, local divisional commanders were then given the discretion to make further advances as far as a line running between the villages of Langemarck and Broodseinde in a possible stage four. A pause for three or four days would then see a follow-up attack seize control of the whole Ypres Ridge between Passchendaele and Staden.

If a stage four was also added, then the advance became 4.5 kilometres in depth, placing it beyond the range of most supporting artillery. At Ypres the more numerous British medium artillery pieces typically had a range of approximately 6000 metres, while the supporting heavy artillery had a range of 9000 metres. From these maximum ranges had to be deducted the gun's location behind the front line which, depending on available space, the tactical situation and the calibre of the gun, meant that the effective planning range for the majority of the artillery pieces was often only several kilometres from the attacking infantry's start line. Gough's plan for day one of the battle was significantly more ambitious than that proposed in the earlier Rawlinson and Plumer versions, where advances to a depth of only 900 to 1600 metres kept the attacking infantry well within range of medium artillery. Despite some doubts among his staff, Haig was prepared to accept the risks inherent in Gough's plan due to its potential for achieving a breakout from the German lines, a potential which accorded with his broader operational vision.

On 31 July the early stages of the attack proceeded to plan. Nine divisions were employed in the attack in the Fifth Army and two in the French First Army, with the thinly held German forward positions rapidly captured with few losses. Valuable ground was gained, including the German observation posts on the highest point of the Gheluvelt Plateau. Despite being badly mauled, the front-line German divisions continued to resist and counter-attacks, supported by artillery fire, soon slowed the Allied advance. The lead divisions of Fifth Army, which had been expected to achieve their phase three (and possibly phase four) objectives by the end of the first day, were now less than halfway to doing so.

Rain had begun to fall on the evening of 31 July and continued unabated for the next three days, only ceasing on 4 August. The heavy falls turned the soil of a badly churned battlefield into a morass. While having an obvious impact on the infantry, the rain also restricted Allied aerial reconnaissance of the German artillery which, in turn, reduced the effectiveness of the Allied counter-battery plan. Resupply of the artillery and infantry also became more difficult as the temporary supply routes to the forward positions were rapidly degraded by high usage and German artillery fire. Considerable engineering resources were allocated to addressing these supply line and communication issues, which helped mitigate the worst of the weather problems until later in the offensive.

Haig visited Gough's Fifth Army Headquarters during the afternoon of 31 July. Despite the failure to achieve the first-day objectives, Haig was optimistic and instructed Gough to continue the advance in accordance with his original plan, but only after adequate bombardment of the German defensive positions and suppression of the German artillery. The British II Corps attack against the German positions on the Gheluvelt Plateau was scheduled to resume on 10 August, while the main offensive would open on 14 August. The II Corps attack on 10 August achieved some initial success, but the infantry could not hold their objectives, as the unsuppressed German artillery isolated the attacking troops, making them vulnerable to German counter-attacks. The failure of the II Corps attack on the Gheluvelt Plateau should have seen a postponement of the 14 August attack since the German artillery located behind the plateau posed a serious threat to continued operations and had yet to be neutralised by counter-battery fire. Haig agreed to a 24-hour delay, but only so that reinforcements could reach the forward troops. To delay further would have jeopardised any chance of conducting the planned amphibious operation on the channel coast since the last high tides finished at the end of August.

THE BATTLE OF LANGEMARCK

While the attack on the morning of 16 August saw the British II and XIX Corps make little progress, further north, XVIII and XIV Corps captured the village of Langemarck and its immediate surrounds. The French First Army also achieved its first-day objectives. Although progress on the northern flank was welcome, the key ground around the Gheluvelt Plateau was still held by the Germans. At a Fifth Army corps commanders' conference on the morning of 17 August, Gough ordered that preparations be made for a resumption of the offensive on 25 August in order to take the ground between the villages of Broodseinde and Westroosebeke. Prior to this attack, the Fifth Army corps commanders were tasked to improve their future lines of departure for the general offensive by conducting local attacks. In particular, the British II Corps was to take Inverness Copse on the Gheluvelt Plateau. The fight for the copse raged from 22 to 24 August, with the Germans ultimately retaining control of the ground. The failure of the II Corps attack marked the end of the third attempt to gain ground on the Gheluvelt Plateau.

By holding the waist of the plateau, German artillery retained its ability to bring down observed fire on Allied positions.

Dissatisfied with Gough's failure to capture the Gheluvelt Plateau, Haig visited Plumer at his Second Army Headquarters on 25 August and proposed that he take back II Corps from Gough, along with the task of capturing the plateau. Haig agreed that Plumer could conduct a series of 'bite and hold' attacks until the line Zandvoorde—Polygon Wood—Broodseinde had been reached. Later that day, back at his own headquarters, Haig restated his decision in the presence of both Gough and Plumer. Plumer was granted three weeks' preparation time before launching his attack, with the British II Corps and its objective now part of Second Army. Because his plan had stalled, Gough's proposal for a major offensive on 25 August was cancelled, although some minor but costly actions associated with the Gough plan continued after this date.

SECOND ARMY RESUMES THE OFFENSIVE

By late August-early September Haig was forced to decide whether to continue the Ypres offensive. Casualty figures between 31 July and 28 August amounted to 3424 officers and 64,586 other ranks killed, wounded or missing. The artillery had expended some 85,396 tons of ammunition and had limited reserves. Faced with heavy losses, diminishing reserves of artillery shells and increasingly bad weather, a decision to halt the offensive would have drawn little criticism from the British government. Lloyd George was eager to halt offensive action for the remainder of 1917 in order to preserve British manpower and despatch forces to support Italy. Haig did not agree with this approach, as he considered that the focus of British efforts should remain on offensive action on the Western Front. To do otherwise would pass the strategic initiative to Germany. Haig also wanted to maintain pressure on the German Army, which he felt was under considerable strain due to heavy battle losses and the impact of Allied artillery and air superiority. Finally, General Pétain urged Haig to continue the offensive to allow the French Army further time to recover, as he doubted the ability of the French to resist the expected German offensive in 1918. In considering all these factors, Haig felt that the arguments for continuing the offensive outweighed the potential risks of higher losses and possible failure.

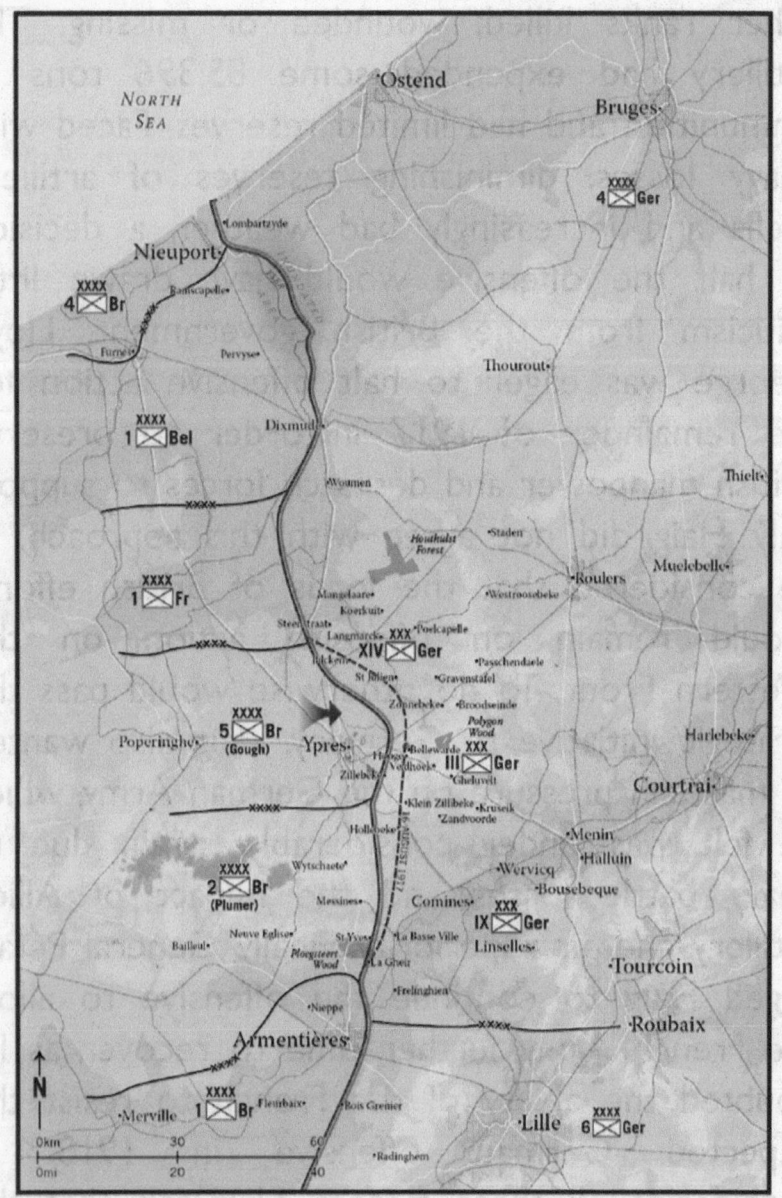

Map 4. The extent of the advance of Gough's Fifth Army following the initial attack on 31 July 1917 and the subsequent attack on Langemarck on 16 August 1917.

FIELD MARSHAL HERBERT CHARLES ONSLOW PLUMER, GCB, GCMC, GCVO, GBE

Born in 1857 in Kensington, London, Herbert Plumer was educated at Eton before going to the Royal Military College, Sandhurst. He was commissioned into the 65th Regiment of Foot in 1876 and went with his battalion to the Sudan in 1884. Plumer attended Staff College, Camberley, from 1886 to 1887, then served in the Cape Colony and Southern Rhodesia. He fought in the Boer War and was promoted to colonel in 1900. In 1902 he was promoted to major general and appointed commander of the 4th Brigade, enjoying a number of divisional commands in the following years. Plumer was sent to France in 1915 and given command of V Corps during the Second Battle of Ypres. He became GOC Second Army in May 1915. Despite some setbacks in the 1916 campaigns, Plumer achieved a major victory at Messines. Haig's confidence in Plumer was reflected in his decision to transfer control of the Third Ypres campaign from Gough's Fifth Army to Plumer's Second Army following Gough's failure at the Battle of Langemarck. In November 1917 Plumer was given command of the British forces sent to the Italian front, subsequently returning to the Western Front to command Second Army during the German Spring Offensive and the Allied Hundred Days campaign. After the war he was promoted to field marshal and held a number of positions including GOC of the British Army of the Rhine, Governor of Malta and High Commissioner of the British Mandate for Palestine. In 1927 he conducted the inaugural ceremony at the Menin Gate, Ypres. He died in London in 1932 and was buried at Westminster Abbey.

Three British Army commanders in conference at Camblainn-Chatelain in 1916. From left, General Sir Herbert Plumer, commanding Second Army, General Sir Edmund Allenby, commanding Third Army and General Sir Henry Horne, commanding First Army (AWM 1108558).

THE BATTLE OF MENIN ROAD

Having received orders to proceed with an attack on the Gheluvelt Plateau, Plumer submitted a plan to Haig on 29 August. Plumer's plan involved four stages, with a planned interval of six days between each stage to allow artillery and supplies to be brought forward before the next stage was launched. Plumer had four divisions (two from X Corps and two from I ANZAC Corps) for the attack in the first stage to a depth of 1300 metres. Compared with Gough's attack on 31 July, the density of Plumer's attacking force had been significantly increased; it would be deployed over less than half the frontage and required to advance less than half the distance. This attacking force was supported by 1339 guns, double the number of guns per division that Gough's plan had provided. In short, Plumer's staged offensive represented a significantly increased concentration of firepower in a series of limited attacks, with the expectation that the culmination of these attacks on limited objectives would achieve what Gough's more ambitious single advance did not. Plumer used the three-week respite granted by Haig to bring forward the artillery and its associated ammunition. The logistic and road networks were repaired and a number of one-way circuits established in the X Corps and I ANZAC Corps areas, since this was where the bulk of the logistic traffic was expected. This process was assisted by a spell of good weather, with the first three weeks of September largely fine with a drying wind.

The first stage of Plumer's attack commenced on 20 September 1917, with the four divisions from X Corps and I ANZAC Corps attacking across the Gheluvelt Plateau towards Gheluvelt itself. Using the Menin Road as an axis of advance, the 1st and 2nd Australian divisions pushed immediately north of Menin Road with the British 23rd and 41st divisions to the south. The two Australian divisions and the British 23rd Division reached their final objectives without significant delays, but the British 41st Division was less fortunate, failing to achieve its final objective, held in check by a cluster of German machine-gun nests known as 'Tower Hamlets'. By midday on 20 September, Second Army had completed the first stage of Plumer's plan. The anticipated German counter-attacks began developing by mid-afternoon, but were disrupted by British artillery and machine-gun barrages. Apart from their posts at Tower Hamlets, the Germans had been driven from their key positions on the Gheluvelt Plateau.

Encouraged by the success at Menin Road, on 21 September Haig authorised the second stage of Plumer's plan. This stage was to be conducted by I ANZAC Corps, which would advance another 1100 metres to capture a line from Polygon Wood to Zonnebeke. To the right of I ANZAC Corps would be the British X Corps, which would continue the advance along Menin Road. On 22 September Haig sent his commanders a map outlining the way he expected the capture of Passchendaele Ridge to unfold. Assuming that the second stage of Plumer's plan was completed by 26 September, Haig intended II ANZAC Corps to move from its reserve position in Second Army and take over the V Corps frontage from Fifth Army. Second Army would then have responsibility for the attack on Passchendaele Ridge. The two ANZAC Corps would then capture Broodseinde, while the British X Corps secured the eastern end of the Gheluvelt Plateau. Finally, Second Army was to occupy the remainder of the northern end of the ridge and capture Passchendaele.

THE BATTLE OF POLYGON WOOD

The second stage of Plumer's plan was launched on 26 September. After three weeks of fine weather, the ground was now so dry that the artillery shells threw up clouds of dust and made navigation difficult for the attacking troops. The 5th and 4th Australian divisions of I ANZAC Corps carried the main thrust of the attack to capture Polygon Wood, with the British X Corps on their right and V Corps (Fifth Army) on their left. The lightly held German forward zone was soon captured and, as at Menin Road, the Allied troops consolidated their positions in anticipation of the German counter-attacks. By mid-afternoon the German attacks had begun to develop, but Allied artillery fire halted them with significant losses. Once again, Plumer's 'bite and hold' tactics had negated the German counter-attack doctrine and resulted in the mauling of at least six German divisions. Their failures at Menin Road and Polygon Wood would lead the Germans to re-evaluate their defensive doctrines for the next battles.

Following the successful battle for Polygon Wood, Haig held a conference on 28 September with Gough and Plumer to consider the next two phases of the offensive. The first would see the capture of the rest of the Gheluvelt Plateau and Broodseinde on Passchendaele Ridge on 4 October. What would happen after this was less certain. Haig believed that there were strong indications that any following phase, to be conducted around 10 October, would offer an opportunity to break through the German lines. With this in mind, he asked both Gough and Plumer to consider this matter. Replying in writing after the conference, both stated that any idea of exploiting a breakthrough into the German lines was premature and could not be considered until the capture of the Passchendaele to Westroosebeke ridge. Haig responded that he did not consider exploitation a necessity for the 10 October attack, but that he wanted his commanders to be ready should the opportunity arise. At a second conference on 2 October, Haig asserted that he was keen not to repeat the German failures of the First Battle of Ypres, where they did not take advantage of British exhaustion to capture the city. Accordingly, Haig ordered each division to hold a brigade in reserve and each corps a division. These units were to be lightly equipped, allocated dedicated artillery and ready to move up to the front line with minimal notice.

THE BATTLE FOR BROODSEINDE

The arrangements for any possible exploitation did not impinge on the conduct of the forthcoming battle, which would be fought in accordance with the now familiar 'bite and hold' tactics. In Second Army two corps, I ANZAC Corps (1st and 2nd Australian divisions) in the south and II ANZAC Corps (3rd Australian Division and New Zealand Division) in the north, were tasked with the capture of Broodseinde and Gravenstafel and their associated heights. Meanwhile, Fifth Army was to attack towards Poelcappelle with four divisions. The proposed date for the operation was 6 October but Haig, fearing a break in the current dry conditions, moved the start date to 4 October. In an attempt to mislead the Germans, Second Army's artillery plan was adjusted so that, apart from counter-battery fire, there would be no preliminary bombardment until zero hour, although barrages were fired on a random basis from 27 September.

The assaulting troops moved into their departure points on the evening of 3 October. By this time the weather had turned, with a strong gale bringing heavy showers. At 5.20am, a German barrage caught the troops from the ANZAC Corps in their exposed positions, causing heavy casualties among the forward brigades. At 6.00am on 4 October the British barrage fell on the German lines, and the ANZAC Corps commenced their assault. Despite the losses from the earlier German barrage, the attack was pressed with conviction and both ANZAC Corps made steady progress against determined German resistance. II ANZAC Corps had the advantage of significantly more artillery than I ANZAC Corps due to the larger frontage of its attack (eight artillery brigades had been transferred from I ANZAC to II ANZAC prior to the attack). By late morning it was clear that significant progress had been made, with both Second Army and Fifth Army capturing large numbers of German prisoners.

Given the obvious success of the attack, Haig's Head of Intelligence went to Plumer's headquarters to discuss whether any attempt should be made to exploit the situation. Because the expected German counter-attack had yet to eventuate, Plumer initially preferred to adhere to the original plan. He maintained that no further advance was possible until the artillery had been brought forward some 3 kilometres. However, by 11.00am he had changed his mind and ordered I ANZAC Corps to push towards the Keiberg spur and II ANZAC Corps to advance up the main ridge towards Passchendaele. While the commander of II ANZAC Corps, Lieutenant General Godley, was in favour of the advance, the commander of I ANZAC Corps, Lieutenant General Birdwood, was not. Birdwood maintained that the fighting had been heavier than anticipated, his artillery could not provide adequate support for any further advance and his supplies were running low. Faced with this advice from Birdwood, by 2.00am Plumer had again changed his mind and reverted to his first preference of remaining with the original plan. The fact that the anticipated German counter-attacks had still not eventuated undoubtedly played on his mind. He was not to know that, as a result of their losses during the Ypres campaign, the German Army had abandoned its previous tactic of committing whole divisions to a counter-attack. At Broodseinde single battalions were fed forward to fill gaps in the line, but the German divisions as a whole were kept in reserve.

CONTINUING THE CAMPAIGN

Steady rain, which began on the afternoon of 4 October, turned into heavy squalls and freezing weather. Despite considerable engineering efforts, the roads and tracks in the area of the battle were now badly churned, making any movement extremely difficult. In some areas, such as the upper reaches of the Steenbeek River behind II ANZAC Corps, conditions had become impossible, described by one divisional engineer as a 'sea of mud'. This had a significant impact on the movement and placement of artillery for the forthcoming Battle of Poelcappelle. Heavy artillery had to be mounted on unstable gun platforms, while field artillery could only advance a short distance from its former positions. Due to the conditions, the artillery batteries were generally located within 100 metres of a main road to facilitate ammunition resupply, with the distance between the road and the guns covered by pack animals. Even with these measures, the artillery could not be resupplied with the quantities of ammunition normally required for a major battle. The ammunition wagons bogged on the poor-quality roads while the pack animals slipped off the plank boardwalks into the mud. Ammunition resupply trips that normally took an hour now took six hours or more. For the infantry, any form of movement was a struggle as they waded through mud up to their knees in places. Not only did this affect their resupply and living conditions but any tactical movements, such as marching from a rear area to their departure trenches prior to the battle, often left the troops exhausted.

Given the severity of the weather, the wisdom of continuing with the impending Poelcappelle and Passchendaele battles remains a point of some contention. In the Australian *Official History*, Bean describes Haig's action to continue with the campaign as the most questioned decision of his career. He wrote that, to the average soldier, the horrendous weather conditions meant that any chance of operational success during the remainder of 1917 had disappeared. There is no doubt that this observation had some validity, as the mud seriously compromised both the mobility and firepower of Haig's divisions in the forthcoming battles. The demands on Haig to discontinue the offensive were not just based on the weather. Since late August, Haig had been under pressure to send troops to support the Allied front in Italy. Added to this, in September the French government asked the British government to take over more of the front line from the French Army.

Despite the weather, and calls to divert his divisions elsewhere, Haig maintained his determination to continue the Ypres offensive. His diary entry of 5 October indicates that he still saw the capture of the Passchendaele—Westroosebeke—Staden ridge as the key to forcing the Germany Army to withdraw from the Belgian coast west of Bruges. Haig's argument for continuing the offensive rested primarily on his belief that the German Army in Flanders was close to breaking. Despite Gough's limited success, Plumer had just completed three 'bite and hold' battles that had resulted in Allied victories. While these battles were won at some cost, the large numbers of German prisoners from the Broodseinde battle seemed to indicate a serious decline in German morale. German losses up to this point are difficult to calculate, but there is little doubt that they had been heavy. General von Kuhl, Chief of Staff to *Army Group Rupprecht,* noted that from 31 July to 20 August at least 17 divisions had been so depleted that they were no longer operationally effective. To Haig, any Allied delay in continuing the attack to Passchendaele would merely provide the German Army a respite to reinforce its depleted divisions and prepare its defences. Time was a critical issue given that German rail resources had only a limited ability to move fresh troops into the Passchendaele area. Any cancellation would also signal the failure of the Ypres campaign to achieve its geographic objectives, something which Haig was not yet prepared to concede.

THE BATTLE OF POELCAPPELLE

The attack on the Passchendaele—Westroosebeke—Staden ridge was to be conducted in two stages. A morning attack by the leading brigades of the attacking divisions would be followed by the reserve brigades in the afternoon. It was hoped that the attack by the reserve brigades would push the German forces beyond Passchendaele, but this latter stage would only occur if the German Army showed signs of retreating. Within Second Army, I ANZAC Corps would attack on the right with the 1st and 2nd Australian divisions leading and the 4th and 5th Australian divisions in reserve. II ANZAC Corps would attack on the left, with the 66th and 49th British divisions leading, and the New Zealand and 3rd Australian divisions in reserve. The boundary between the two corps was the Ypres to Roulers rail line.

The attack was planned for 9 October 1917, despite the fact that the rain had continued unabated since 4 October. At a conference on 7 October, Plumer and Gough advised Haig that they would welcome an end to the offensive, but would continue if required. Haig agreed to cancel the proposed afternoon stage of the attack, but wanted at the very least to drive the Germans from the Passchendaele—Westroosebeke portion of the ridge. During the night of 7 October the rain ceased, only to recommence on the morning of 8 October.

After a difficult night tramping through the mud to the start line, the infantry attacked at 5.20am on the morning of 9 October. Because of their unstable gun platforms and lack of ammunition, the barrage was not as effective as the 'bite and hold' tactics required. Given the central importance of artillery to these tactics, it is hardly surprising that the attack generally made little headway. In many places the German wire was not cut and machine-gun nests remained unsuppressed. Ravebeek Creek, south-east of Passchendaele, was now a morass of waist-deep water some 25 to 40 metres wide, a significant obstacle which few men managed to cross. Progress was more rapid for those troops on the sandy ground close to the top of Passchendaele Ridge. British troops from the 66th Division reached Passchendaele by midday but, believing they had no flank support, subsequently withdrew.

By the end of the day the gains made by the attack were small—indeed, so insignificant was the ground taken that the British *Official History* provided no dedicated map for this battle. However the fact that troops had reached Passchendaele at all must have been a source of optimism. On the evening of 9 October Plumer informed Haig's headquarters that, in his opinion, the ground gained by II ANZAC Corps was sufficient to provide a start line for another attack on 12 October—an attack which Plumer felt had a reasonable possibility of capturing

Passchendaele. Having been held in reserve for the Poelcappelle attack, the New Zealand Division and the 3rd Australian Division now moved up to the front line in preparation for the 12 October attack.

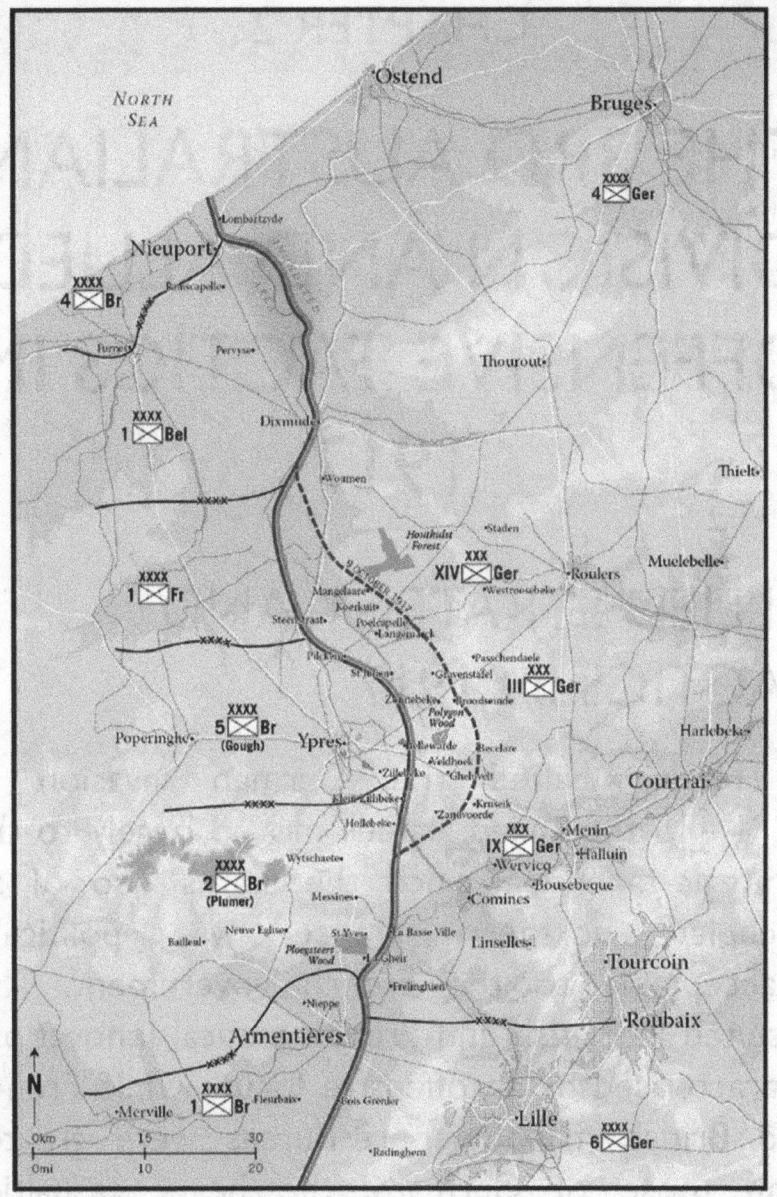

Map 5. Ground captured by Plumer's Second Army during the battles of Menin Road, Polygon Wood, Broodseinde and Poelcappelle up to 9 October 1917.

CHAPTER 2

THE 3RD AUSTRALIAN DIVISION AND ALLIED OFFENSIVE TACTICS IN 1917

ALLIED STRATEGY AND TACTICS IN 1917

Having halted the German invasion in 1914—15 the Allied armies moved largely to the strategic offensive, since the status quo of an occupied northern France was politically unacceptable to the French government. This resulted in British and French tactical innovations characterised by an offensive focus. While French and British manpower resources were greater than those of Germany, the heavy casualties sustained by the BEF on the Somme and the French Army at Verdun were militarily and politically unsustainable. Thus, the problem confronting BEF and Australian headquarters staff in 1917 was how best to pursue offensive action while keeping casualties to a minimum. In short, they were faced with devising the best tactics to achieve their most basic task—that of crossing no man's land and capturing the opposing German trenches. Likewise, they needed to ensure that such an attack would also destroy or capture the defending German forces and then hold the captured ground against German counter-attacks.

Two major factors militated against a successful crossing of no man's land by Allied infantry. The first of these factors was barbed-wire obstacles and these could be formidable. Until the tank provided an alternative means of crossing barbed wire, the only way it could be removed prior to an attack was by shelling. The extensive shelling required for the breaching of barbed wire created further obstacles. In areas such as Flanders, with its high water table and vulnerable drainage systems, the churned landscape invariably turned to mud with the first rains. Such conditions, while not preventing the infantry crossing no man's land, certainly slowed assaulting troops.

The second major factor impeding any attack was German firepower. This could be delivered by rifle, machine-gun or artillery—and usually all three in combination. While the machine-gun is generally recognised as the weapon that instigated trench warfare, artillery fire was the most effective killer and, by war's end, had inflicted some 60% of all front-line casualties. However machine-guns continued to play a vital role since their sustained direct fire reinforced the effectiveness of the barbed-wire obstacle. For any attacking infantry, attempting to cut through barbed-wire obstacles while under machine-gun fire was at best a slow task and at worst suicidal.

BARBED WIRE

A view of the multiple belts of barbed wire typically erected in front of a German defensive line, in this case the Hindenburg Line in October 1918 (AWM E03481).

Under British doctrine, the first strands of barbed wire were erected some 18 metres from the forward trench line with a depth of at least 9 metres. The wire could be up to a height of 2 metres, with every effort made to conceal it in folds of dead ground, placing it below the attacker's line of sight and the defender's line of fire. Where possible, a second belt of wire to the same depth would be constructed some 35 to 45 metres from the friendly trench line in order to keep grenade throwers at a safe distance. German wire followed the same basic principles as the British, but with some variation. Where possible, two or three belts of barbed-wire obstacles were constructed, each 3 to 5 metres wide, with a gap of 5 to 6 metres between the belts. These gaps were generally filled with low trip wire, pointed stakes and occasional wire entanglements connecting the main belts. If multiple belts could not be constructed, then a single belt with a width of 15 to 20 metres would be erected. Where possible the barbed wire was supported by steel posts that screwed into the ground. These steel posts were not only more durable than wooden posts, but had the added advantage of being less visible and could be inserted into the ground by a man lying down using a crowbar. When the opportunity arose, such as in front of the German Hindenburg Line, more extensive belts of wire were erected beyond the basic obstacles outlined above.

In many ways, the narrative of Allied tactics aimed at cracking the German defences was the story of artillery tactics. The British Army had learnt a number of painful lessons in 1915—16 concerning the employment of artillery, the most important of these that an infantry attack without sufficient artillery support was doomed to failure. By 1917 the ratio of artillery pieces and rounds per metre of contested ground had been reduced to the status of a mathematical formula. The ability to implement this formula was contingent on the provision of sufficient guns, a continuous supply of shells and the staff skills to properly control and coordinate this firepower. The predominance of artillery in tactical thinking gradually produced doctrine that advocated massive shelling of the German trench line prior to any attack. Such doctrine was based on the belief that artillery could destroy almost all German troops in their front-line trenches, requiring the advancing infantry to merely occupy the devastated objective. In effect, the use of massed artillery would restore a degree of mobility to the battlefield by destroying the very machine-guns and barbed wire that had removed it in the first place. The only element of German defensive firepower that remained was the opposing German artillery. While the necessary techniques to destroy the German artillery through effective counter-battery fire, particularly the reconnaissance and surveying skills for accurate predictive fire, took longer to develop, by the time of the Third Ypres offensive the BEF had the necessary capability in place.

Inevitably there were disadvantages in this artillery-based doctrine of total destruction. Primarily, it removed any chance of operational surprise, since the many days of shelling required to achieve total destruction alerted the German defences as to where the impending attack was to take place. This enabled the Germans to position their reserves out of artillery range, allowing them to either conduct counter-attacks to recapture their lost trenches or be used to contain the incursion. The massed shelling also destroyed the road and rail systems within the immediate area of the attack. This made rapid movement off the battlefield difficult, restricting the ability of the infantry or cavalry to exploit beyond the initially captured German trench lines. In addition, since BEF forces had to move through the battlefield to reach open country, their ability to reinforce any breakthrough was slower than the German Army's ability to contain it. The Germans could use their rail system and interior lines of communication outside the battle zone to rapidly move troops to contain any breakthrough. Finally, the doctrine placed a premium on a cautious and methodological approach to battle planning, where exploitation was a function of how quickly artillery could be moved forward. While it offered a solution for the destruction of German barbed wire and the neutralisation of German firepower, its very success also contained the germ of its own limitations since exploitation of any initial attack was extremely difficult. Seen in this light, Haig's initial choice to select Gough's more ambitious offensive plan which moved beyond the limitations of the 'bite and hold' tactics is understandable.

Alongside these developments in artillery tactics, infantry and artillery cooperation also experienced a dramatic change from 1916 to 1917. In 1916 barrages employed in support of infantry attacks were either 'standing' barrages used to block a potential German avenue of counter-attack, or 'lifting' barrages which would move from one target to the next in accordance with a predetermined plan. A third type of barrage which appeared in 1916 was the 'creeping' barrage, designed to advance at a steady rate, just in front of the advancing infantry.

These three types of barrages all lacked flexibility in that, if the infantry did not conform to the timings or rates of advance specified in the divisional or corps fire plan, its impact was significantly diminished and the attacking troops could be left dangerously exposed. There was an increased recognition that the artillery Forward Observation Officer (FOO), used to control the application of artillery fire on the front line, needed to be more responsive to the requirements of the infantry. By mid-1917 FOOs and their signal parties were assigned to attacking battalions and were beginning to move forward with their infantry, providing intimate fire control support to their assigned troops. This practice, when combined with the tactic of providing the FOO with an artillery 'reserve' which he could switch from one target to another, enabled artillery to be far more responsive to the rhythms of battle.

By 1916 the organisation, personal equipment and weapons of the Australian divisions had reached the standard required to fight and survive on the Western Front. Invariably this meant closely conforming to the establishment and equipment of their British counterparts. This was particularly so for divisional artillery, which meant that, by 1917, Australian divisions had supplemented their firepower with heavy, medium and light mortar companies. These mortars, when combined with the two artillery brigades of howitzers, field guns and medium machine-guns (now consolidated into a company within the infantry brigade capable of providing machine-gun barrage fire) made the 1917 War Establishment of an AIF division a formidable organisation, capable of generating a significant amount of direct and indirect firepower. The effective use of this firepower relied on experienced divisional staff officers with the skills to integrate the divisional firepower with the supporting arms and services external to the division, such as corps artillery, signals, logistics and the rapidly developing air and tank capabilities

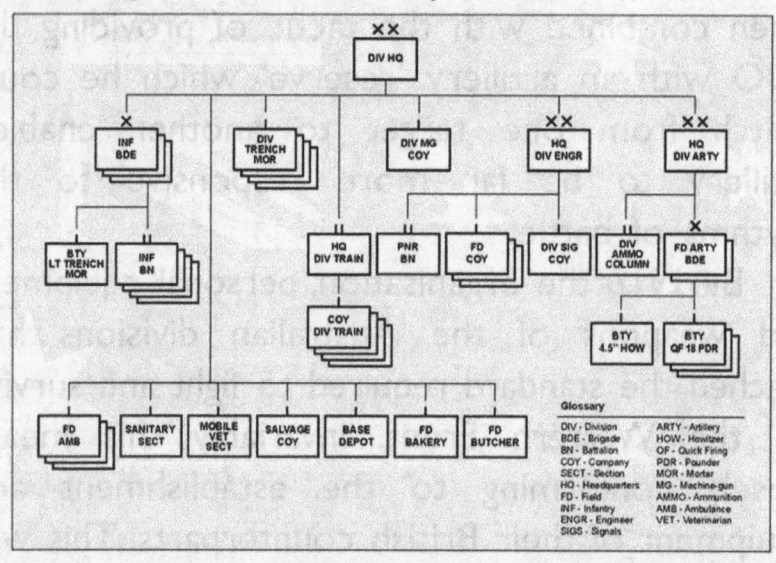

Diagram 1. The organisation of an Australian infantry division in 1917.

Headquarters:	Headquarters 3rd Division
Artillery:	Headquarters 3rd Division Artillery
	3rd Division Ammunition Column
	1, 2, 3, 4, Sections
	3rd Australian Division Trench Mortars
	V3A Heavy Trench Mortar Battery
	X3A Medium Trench Mortar Battery
	Y3A Medium Trench Mortar Battery
	Z3A Medium Trench Mortar Battery
	Headquarters 7th Field Artillery Brigade
	25th, 26th, 27th Batteries
	10th Howitzer Battery
	Headquarters 8th Field Artillery Brigade
	29th, 30th, 31st Batteries
	108th Howitzer Battery
Engineers:	Headquarters 3rd Divisional Engineers
	9th, 10th, 11th, Field Companies
	3rd Divisional Signal Company
	3rd Australian Pioneer Battalion
Infantry:	Headquarters 9th Infantry Brigade
	33rd Battalion, The New England Regiment
	34th Battalion, The Illawarra Regiment
	35th Battalion, Newcastle's Own Regiment
	36th Battalion, St George's English Rifle Regiment
	9th Australian Light Trench Mortar Battery
	Headquarters 10th Infantry Brigade
	37th Battalion, The Henty Regiment
	38th Battalion, The Northern Victoria Regiment
	39th Battalion, The Hawthorn-Kew Regiment
	40th Battalion, The Derwent Regiment
	10th Australian Light Trench Mortar Battery
	Headquarters 11th Infantry Brigade
	41st Battalion, The Byron Scottish
	42nd Battalion, The Capricornia Regiment
	43rd Battalion, The Hindmarsh Regiment
	44th Battalion, The West Australian Rifles
	11th Australian Light Trench Mortar battery
Machine-Gun:	3rd Australian Machine Gun Company
Transport:	Headquarters 3rd Australian Divisional Train
	22nd, 23rd, 24th, 25th Companies
Medical:	9th, 10th, 11th Field Ambulances
	3rd Australian Sanitary Section
Veterinary:	3rd Australian Mobile Veterinary Section
Other:	3rd Australian Division Salvage Company
	3rd Australian Division Base Depot
	3rd Australian Division Field Bakery
	3rd Australian Division Field Butchery

Diagram 2. Units of the 3rd Australian Division in 1917.

Innovation was not just confined to the artillery arm of the division. By 1916 the basic organisational unit of an infantry brigade, the battalion, had seen an increase in size and capability from the battalion of 1915. The 1916 battalion had gained a number of specialist units, reflecting the lessons of combat on the Western Front. These included Bombing (hand grenade), Rifle Bombing and Lewis sections within the platoon. The Lewis gun was first introduced into Australian divisions in 1916 in the form of a Lewis machine-gun section of four guns per battalion. Given their limited distribution, they were centrally managed as a battalion resource, partly as compensation for the loss of Vickers medium machine-guns, which had been removed to form brigade-level machine-gun companies. While the number of Lewis guns slowly increased within the battalion, it was not until 1917 that sufficient numbers were produced to equip the companies of the battalion with their own guns. The addition of a Lewis gun section and two bombing sections within the infantry platoon provided the basis for a significant change in the way the platoon fought. Unlike the much heavier Vickers machine-gun, the Lewis gun could manoeuvre with the attacking infantry platoon as an integral part of the unit's firepower. The Lewis gun could lay down suppressing fire on a German position, enabling soldiers equipped with Mills bombs to close with the position and destroy it. Launching Mills bombs from the standard Lee

Enfield rifle, in the form of a rifle grenade, at German bunkers and machine-gun nests also allowed the infantry to complete this destruction from a distance, further reducing the risks associated with closing with the enemy.

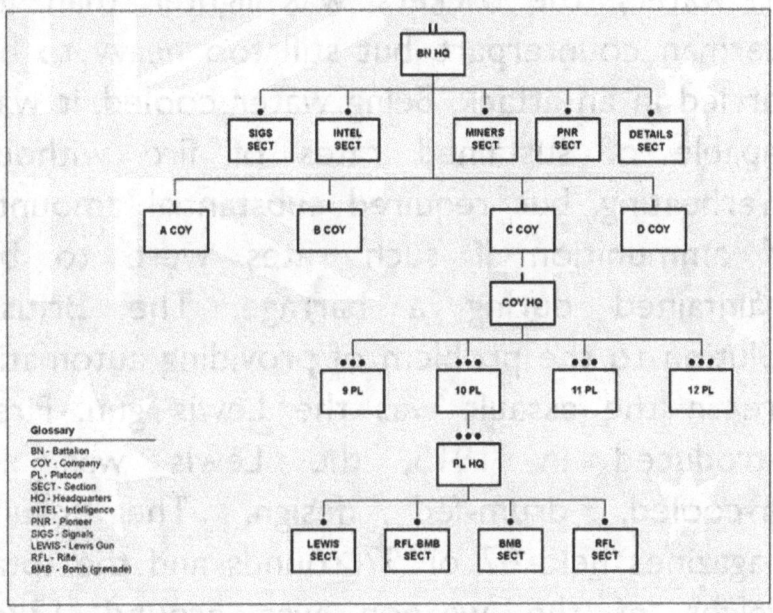

Diagram 3. The organisation of an Australian infantry battalion in 1917.

THE VICKERS MEDIUM MACHINE-GUN MK I AND THE LEWIS LIGHT MACHINE-GUN, MK I

The standard medium machine-gun for all BEF forces, the Vickers MK I, was a belt-fed, water-cooled weapon with an effective range of 1800 metres and a maximum rate of fire of 600 rounds per minute. It fired a .303-inch

(7.7mm) round, the same type used in the standard BEF infantry rifle, the Short Magazine Lee-Enfield No.1, Mk III and in the Lewis gun. With a weight of 18kg (excluding ammunition or water), the Vickers was lighter than its German counterpart, but still too heavy to be carried in an attack. Being water cooled, it was capable of sustained rates of fire without overheating, but required substantial amounts of ammunition if such rates were to be maintained during a barrage. The British solution to the problem of providing automatic fire in the assault was the Lewis gun. First introduced in 1915, the Lewis was an air-cooled, drum-fed design. The drum magazines held 47 or 97 rounds and the total weight of the weapon was around 13kg, approximately half that of its medium machine-gun contemporaries. Effective range was 800 metres and the Lewis was generally fired in short bursts. In the 1917 British pamphlet *S.S. 201, The Tactical Summary of Machine Gun Operations*, emphasis was placed on the need to integrate the different characteristics and firepower of these two weapons in all aspects of attack and defence. The Lewis gun was regarded as 'the natural link between the Vickers Gun and the infantry'.

For example, in an attack the Vickers would maintain a sustained, overhead, frontal fire on the German positions while the Lewis guns were deployed to the flanks or rear. By coordinating the fires of these two weapons, the BEF had the means to provide automatic covering fire for the infantry right onto the German positions which could then be taken by grenade or bayonet.

Soldiers and officers from the 4th Australian Machine Gun Company conduct a practice shoot with the Vickers medium machine-gun Mk I in 1917 (AWM P02670.007).

Soldiers from the 28th Battalion training with the Lewis light machine-gun in 1917 (AWM E00683).

The tactical changes—and resulting organisational changes within the platoon in 1917—were a combination of two factors. The first was combat experience within the platoon itself and saw the soldiers work out how to employ the weapons to achieve maximum effect while restricting their own losses. The second was the need for BEF headquarters staff to capture and then codify into doctrine the lessons of their 1916 battles and those of the French Army. The resulting confluence of these two forces was the publication by Haig's General

Headquarters of the pamphlet *S.S. 143, Instructions for the Training of Platoons for Offensive Action* in early 1917. This pamphlet established the newly restructured platoon as the basic offensive unit within the company and, by March 1917, the majority of AIF divisions were restructured to conform to this requirement. Other pamphlets soon followed, describing the changes wrought within the battalion and how the battalion would now conduct an attack. The *S.S.143* pamphlet set the structure of minor infantry tactics for the remainder of the war.

RAISING AND TRAINING THE 3RD AUSTRALIAN DIVISION

Following its return to Egypt from the Gallipoli campaign the AIF underwent a significant expansion and reorganisation, growing from the existing two divisions (1st and 2nd) and two independent brigades (4th and 8th brigades) to five Australian divisions and associated Light Horse brigades. The 4th and 5th divisions were formed in Egypt, while the 3rd Division was raised in Australia. Like the original divisions, the 3rd Division was recruited on a regional basis. The 9th Brigade comprised the 33rd to 36th battalions, recruited from New South Wales; the 10th Brigade, with the 37th to 39th battalions, was recruited from Victoria; while the 40th Battalion came from Tasmania. The 11th Brigade, with its 41st and 42nd battalions, came from Queensland, the 43rd Battalion from South Australia and the 44th Battalion from Western Australia. The supporting arms and services of the division were also raised on a similar regional basis. The units of the division completed limited basic training in Australia before individually embarking on a six-week sea voyage for the divisional camp at Lark Hill on the windswept Salisbury Plain in England.

Being raised in Australia from raw recruits meant that, unlike its newly raised sister divisions in Egypt, the 3rd Australian Division did not benefit from an experienced cadre of troops. This, plus the fact that the division's soldiers had not enlisted on the declaration of war, set them apart from the rest of the AIF. Alluding to their delayed enlistment, other AIF soldiers would later apply disparaging nicknames to members of the division, including the 'procrastinators', the 'hard thinkers' or 'the neutrals'. Unit training in Australia was rudimentary and of an inconsistent standard, making the division unsuitable for deployment in France. The division's new commanding officer, the recently promoted Major General John Monash, was an experienced brigade commander (having relinquished command of the

4th Brigade) and immediately recognised this deficiency. In a letter to his wife in August 1916, Monash stated that his first task as a commander was to start the division on a program of systematic organisation and training. He estimated that this would take at least six weeks, but also noted (prophetically) that it could take much longer.

Monash instigated a 13-week unit training program that would see collective training escalate from company to battalion, then from battalion to brigade and finally to divisional-level training and exercises. His aim was to introduce standardised combat tactics and procedures into the division that would enhance cooperation among units at all levels of command. The skills of individual specialists, such as signallers, engineers or gunners, would be developed by sending Australian soldiers to British training schools. Once qualified, these newly trained soldiers would form a pool of specialists who would then conduct training courses within the division. One area in which the 3rd Australian Division was seriously deficient (like the majority of AIF divisions) was in the number of qualified Australian staff officers. The initial staff officers within the Divisional Headquarters were predominately English and Indian Army officers and it was not until 1917 that the AIF had developed sufficient expertise to start to fill these critical, if often unglamorous positions.

Having previously commanded troops on the Western Front, Monash had an appreciation for the importance of training in building a successful division. He also recognised that such training had to be relevant to the conditions in which his troops would fight. With only limited experience from the Gallipoli campaign (much of which was not relevant to the Western Front), the Australian Army readily adopted British weapons, organisation, tactics and doctrine. This was not a forced relationship. While there has been a modern Australian propensity to emphasise the differences between the AIF and the British Army, in reality such differences were constrained. The AIF was primarily raised and equipped according to British Army organisational tables and relied heavily on British support in all areas of equipment, supply and organisation. While AIF commanders such as Monash were permitted some latitude in the way they trained their divisions, the general doctrine under which they were trained was determined by Haig's headquarters down through his subordinate corps headquarters. This was hardly surprising. In the industrialised, mass conflict that the Western Front had become, an emphasis on standardised doctrine, organisation and procedures was essential if the divisions and corps of the BEF, drawn from all areas of the British Empire, were to work together successfully.

Throughout 1916 Monash, an enthusiastic trainer of troops, had made systematic efforts to indoctrinate his division in the latest tactics through realistic training. George Cuttriss, a chaplain with the 43rd Infantry Battalion, wrote of Monash:

> He is a popular and painstaking officer, a born leader, a strict disciplinarian, possessed of tireless energy. He has not spared himself in his efforts to establish and maintain a high standard of efficiency amongst all ranks. The G.O.C. set himself to put his men right and succeeded. He has a wonderfully comprehensive grip over every branch of activity, and woe betide the officer or man who was indifferent to or negligent of the duties entrusted to him.

GENERAL SIR JOHN MONASH, GCMG, KCB, VD

John Monash was born in Melbourne in 1865 to parents of Prussian-Jewish origin. Educated at Scotch College and the University of Melbourne, he graduated in engineering in 1893 and arts/law in 1895. In 1884 he joined the University Company of the 4th Battalion, Victoria Rifles, transferring to the North Melbourne Battery of the Garrison Artillery in 1866, becoming a battery commander in 1896. In 1913 he was promoted to colonel and given command of the 13th Brigade. With the outbreak of war Monash was appointed to command of the AIF 4th Brigade and took part in the Gallipoli campaign. Following the AIF withdrawal from Gallipoli, Monash spent time training his brigade in Egypt before both were transferred to the Western Front in June 1916. At this time Monash was promoted to major general and given command of the 3rd Australian Division, spending five months training his division on Salisbury Plain. Monash commanded his division through the battles of Messines, Broodseinde and First Passchendaele. In May 1918 he was promoted to lieutenant general and took over from General Birdwood as operational commander of the Australian Corps, Birdwood retaining administrative command of the Corps until the end of the war. Monash commanded the Australian Corps at the battles of Hamel, Amiens, Chuignes, Mont St Quentin, Péronne, Hargicourt and the Hindenburg Line. At the end of the war he was appointed Director-General of Repatriation and Demobilisation and oversaw the repatriation of 160,000 Australian troops before returning to Australia in December 1919. Monash was placed on the Army Unattached List on 1 January 1920 and held a number of prominent positions, including Head of the State Electricity Commission of Victoria and Vice-Chancellor of Melbourne University. Among other activities, he promoted and oversaw the construction of the Shrine of Remembrance in Melbourne. Monash died in 1931 at the age of 66. He was granted a state funeral and buried in Brighton General Cemetery, Melbourne.

Portrait of General Sir John Monash in 1919 by John Longstaff (AWM ART02986).

Group portrait of the 3rd Australian Division Headquarters staff taken at Lark Hill, Wiltshire, in November 1916, prior to their embarkation for France. Monash is seated in the centre of the front row. Of his six principal staff officers sitting in the front row, three were from the British Army (AWM A01584).

While the division lacked combat experience, once it arrived in France in November 1916 Monash wasted few opportunities to remedy this deficiency. Occupying the line in the Armentières sector, the division spent its first winter practising trench raids, becoming so proficient in this art form that Bean soon considered the men of the 3rd Division more experienced at raiding than any other Australian division. Such raids were not only conducted at battalion level and below, but also at brigade level, with large-scale raids planned and conducted in March 1917.

The Battle of Messines was the 3rd Division's first major action. Responsible for the right flank of the attack as part of II ANZAC Corps, Monash deployed two brigades in the attack, each with two battalions forward. The role of the 3rd Division was daunting for such a relatively inexperienced formation, but Monash's attention to detail was evident in its preparation. After obtaining their proposed plans of attack from his brigade commanders, Monash personally worked out a detailed program describing how each battalion would fight, even extending as far as the deployment of some platoons and sections. By the time the division's operational order for the battle had been issued the plan had been elaborated in 36 successive circulars, with instructions for the employment of some sub-units, such as the divisional machine-guns, occupying multiple parts.

Brigade rehearsals were conducted and orders delivered down to company and platoon level in front of large-scale models of the battlefield. However, even such meticulous attention to detail could not avert risks from unexpected German action. On 6 June 1917 the division suffered over 2000 casualties from a German gas barrage that struck during the approach march to the line of departure for the division's attack at Messines. During the actual assault, casualties were relatively light and the lead battalions (33rd, 34th, 38th and 39th) gained their objectives with minimal opposition.

Following Messines the division enjoyed a rest in a relatively quiet sector and received reinforcements to replace the losses suffered in the battle. Conditions further improved when, in August 1917, the division was removed from the line and sent to a Second Army rest area close to St Omer. With the Ypres offensive in full flight since 31 July, the division's absence from battle would only be temporary. On 22 September Haig inspected 12,000 soldiers of the 3rd Division on parade and the next day Monash received orders for the division to return to the front line at Ypres to take part in what would be the Battle of Broodseinde. While this would require the men to complete a five-day route march, Monash considered his men fully rested and fit and his division at full strength for the coming battles.

Monash's plan of attack at Broodseinde involved two brigades leading, with the 10th on the left and the 11th on the right. The attack was launched on 4 October and, as at Messines, the unfortunate division was again caught in the open by a German barrage fired immediately prior to zero hour, this time as part of a German attack. Following bitter hand-to-hand fighting in no man's land, German resistance crumbled and, some three hours after zero hour, the division had secured its objectives for the loss of 1810 casualties. In his planning for Broodseinde Monash again exhibited that close attention to detail he had displayed at Messines, specifying certain actions down to platoon and company level. While such detailed supervision was understandable for Messines where, apart from trench raids, his command team was largely untested in the conduct of a divisional attack, it was less so at Broodseinde. Detailed planning certainly had its advantages when dealing with inexperienced troops, but with experienced soldiers, as those of the 3rd Division now were, detailed orders restricted the troops' ability to exercise their own initiative.

Three days after the battle the division was rotated out of the line for a rest. Second Army attacked Poelcappelle again on 9 October, but the 3rd Australian Division remained in reserve. As it readied itself for its fateful attack on Passchendaele on 12 October, it is useful to take stock of the division's status. Despite having suffered over 3000 casualties since June, it had successfully attacked and captured a series of well-constructed German defensive lines. In

Monash, the division had a talented commander. He had a personal tendency to over-manage his division, but within the tactical restrictions of the 'bite and hold' battle such a tendency was not the disadvantage it could have been in the more fluid conditions of the Palestine campaign, for example. More importantly, Monash had a solid grasp of 1917 tactical doctrine and how it should be employed. He had also taken measures to implement a regime that ensured the 3rd Division actually practised the latest developments in Allied tactical doctrine. The battles of Messines and Broodseinde had also provided the division with combat experience and, despite its losses, any objective assessment of the division on the eve of Passchendaele would have rated it a capable and experienced formation.

CHAPTER 3

THE 195TH GERMAN INFANTRY DIVISION AND GERMAN DEFENSIVE TACTICS IN 1917

THE GERMAN STRATEGIC PICTURE ON THE WESTERN FRONT IN 1917

The problems facing the German Army in 1917 were formidable. While the Eastern Front still offered opportunities for offensive action, in the west the Army was on the strategic defensive. The 1916 battles of Verdun and the Somme inflicted heavy losses on German forces and significantly depleted their reserves of manpower. While any Russian capitulation would release German divisions for the Western Front, there was no immediate prospect of such a collapse. An additional risk was the German declaration of unrestricted submarine warfare in January 1917. While Germany hoped that its U-boat campaign would prove decisive and bring victory in 1917, it also had the potential to bring America into the war on the side of the Allies. Should this happen while Russia remained undefeated, the German Army would be even more outnumbered on the Western Front.

As it stood, in August 1916 German intelligence estimated that it faced 58 BEF divisions and 110 French divisions, with France having the potential to raise another 10 or 11 divisions. In November 1916 the German Army had some 121 divisions on the Western Front (76 in Russia and Rumania), an increase from 112 in July 1916. This increase had commenced under Field Marshal Eric von Falkenhayn who planned to raise 18 new divisions using the expedient measure of reducing the number of infantry regiments in each German division from four to three. However by late 1916 demography dictated that the German deficit in divisions on the Western Front could only grow while Russia remained in the war. When compared to the Allied nations, the German population base was too small to sustain the creation of additional divisions as well as provide manpower to meet the requirements of other sectors such as the armaments industry.

GERMAN ARTILLERY: M1916 77MM FIELD GUN AND M1916 105MM LIGHT FIELD HOWITZER

The German Army employed a wide variety of artillery pieces in the light, medium and heavy range, including howitzers and mortars of all descriptions. By 1917 it had standardised its artillery to eight pieces which formed the core of its fire support. Two of the base weapons were the M1916 77mm field gun and the M1916 105mm light field howitzer, the German equivalent of the ubiquitous British QF18-pounder and the QF 4.5-inch howitzer. The M1916 77mm field gun was a development of an earlier 1896 weapon and fired a 7.2kg (16lb) shell of 77mm (3-inch) calibre to an effective range of 9100 metres. The M1916 light field howitzer was also developed from an earlier artillery piece and was mounted on the same gun carriage as the field gun. The howitzer fired a 14.8kg (32.7lb) shell of 105mm (4.1-inch) calibre to a maximum range of 9225 metres. As trench warfare developed, the ratio of German Army howitzers to field guns increased significantly, as the tactical advantages of howitzers lobbing shells into concealed positions became obvious. Like the BEF, German artillery doctrine also evolved during the course of the war and the Germans generally led the Allies in the development of artillery tactics and equipment for defensive operations—particularly in the use of gas and neutralisation barrages. While German artillery pieces were often technically superior to their Allied counterparts in the medium and heavy artillery categories, at least until 1916, this did little to compensate for Allied numerical superiority.

A captured German 77mm gun (AWM C04667).

A captured German 105mm howitzer (AWM P00520.016).

Another area of concern for the German Army lay in the production of artillery and munitions. Just as artillery was the principal offensive weapon for the BEF, for the German Army it provided the foundation for any successful defence. The battles of 1916 had seen prodigious quantities of munitions expended by German artillery. In the Somme, between July and August 1916, the German Army had expended 587 field artillery munitions trains and 372 heavy artillery munitions trains (one train delivered 26,880 77mm rounds, 12,000 105mm rounds or 6000 150mm rounds). German munitions production was hampered by the lack of natural nitrate propellant for shells which initially had been imported from abroad. The Allied naval blockade cut off this supply and forced German industry to switch to the production of synthetic nitrates, but by 1916 such production was only covering existing munitions demands. After taking command of the German forces on the Western Front in August 1916, Field Marshal Paul von Hindenburg and General Erich von Ludendorff implemented a program to significantly expand artillery, machine-gun and trench mortar production. While a necessary requirement for the equipping of the new German divisions, Hindenburg and Ludendorff also saw an expansion of divisional firepower as a substitute for German manpower shortages. But the restrictions on German industry in nitrate and armaments production meant that any proposed artillery expansion would not only be limited, but would also adversely affect the strength of the German field army. Indeed, by November 1916 some two million skilled workers had to be withdrawn from the Army to serve in German industry, exacerbating the very issue that artillery and munitions expansion was supposed to alleviate.

THE SEARCH FOR A SUCCESSFUL DEFENSIVE DOCTRINE

Faced with numerical inferiority, in an environment that could deplete manpower at a rapid rate (the Somme battles alone destroying the manpower equivalent of 95.5 German divisions), the German Army desperately needed a tactical solution to the problem of Allied superiority in manpower and artillery. While the Hindenburg-Ludendorff rearmament plan achieved an increase in the firepower of the German divisions, they still lagged behind their Allied counterparts. Even had this not been the case, material improvements in equipment could only go so far in compensating for German numerical inferiority. The only feasible avenue open to the German Army to address its strategic conundrum was the development of a viable defensive doctrine—one which could defeat the increasing dominance of the Allied evolving 'bite and hold' tactics.

Before he was replaced by Hindenburg and Ludendorff, Falkenhayn had begun the process of writing and distributing manuals on defensive tactics entitled *Instruction for Position Warfare for All Arms*. While Falkenhayn favoured a rigid defence of the front line, these manuals initiated the Army's move away from the concept of holding the forward trenches at all costs to one of defence in depth. The battles of 1915 and 1916 had made it clear that holding the forward trenches in strength only played to the Allied advantage in artillery, since it concentrated German defensive manpower in a limited area. Defence in depth dispersed defensive manpower, complicated Allied fire planning and enabled the front line to be held by just a small number of troops. The new defence would be built not on defensive lines, but on a collection of fortified positions designed to absorb and then entrap any Allied attack. Lost territory would then be retaken by a local counter-attack or, if a larger force was required, by a deliberate attack in divisional strength or greater. Ludendorff also advocated giving the local defence commander (usually a battalion commander and designated Commander of the Forward Troops) greater autonomy in how to conduct his own defence. The local defence commander had the support of his regimental commander for logistics, but would not be under his superior's direct control when deciding how the defensive battle would be fought. Any reinforcements fed into the defensive battle would also come under the authority of the local defence commander. If the attack was of such magnitude that a battalion commander could no longer control the battle, then the divisional commander and his staff would assume the role of the local defence commander and fight the battle on behalf of the corps commander.

Such changes were not readily accepted in a hierarchical army, particularly the concept of local commanders having the authority to fight the defensive battle rather than their immediate superiors. Nevertheless the ideas of flexible defence and decentralised command of the defensive battle were eventually incorporated into the existing German manuals on positional warfare. A new manual, entitled *The Principles of Command in the Defensive Battle in Position Warfare*, stated that the aim of the German defence was to compel the Allied attacking force to fight itself to a standstill and deplete its resources in men, while the defenders conserved their strength. The defence was not to be based on the employment of the largest number of men, but would principally rely on firepower from artillery, trench mortars and machine-guns. Furthermore, the defence would only be conducted under conditions favourable to the Germans and ground would be relinquished if Allied pressure made this necessary. If the Allied attack penetrated the local defences, the local general reserve would conduct a quick counter-attack. Should this prove insufficient to remove the attacker, then a more methodical (usually divisional-level) attack would be conducted. Finally, the primary role for the corps and army headquarters in this doctrine was to set out guiding principles for the preparation of the battle. The battle itself would be fought by the front-line infantry divisions which would be given independence of action within their own sectors, but within the guidelines set by corps.

Once *The Principles of Command in the Defensive Battle in Position Warfare* became widely distributed and accepted, the German Army produced detailed operating procedures describing how the defence would be conducted. During the latter stages of the Ypres campaign, a German battalion tasked to defend a sector of the line would operate with three defensive zones: an Outpost Line, a Forward Zone and a Main Line of Resistance. The bulk of the battalion's companies would be positioned in the Main Line of Resistance, with one or two platoons and a machine-gun occupying the Forward Zone some 500 metres from the Main Line of Resistance. The Forward Zone was tasked with repelling Allied patrols and providing resistance short of a major attack, with the troops deployed in a chequerboard fashion. The

Outpost Line, itself closer to the Allied trenches than the Forward Zone, would act as an early warning system for the entire battalion and delineated the furthest extent of the German line in the Forward Zone. Should warning be received of a major Allied attack, then the troops in the Forward Zone would retreat to the Main Line of Resistance to escape the bombardment. The Germans calculated that a typical British barrage had a depth of some 540 metres. By forcing the British barrage to first fire on the Forward Zone, German Forward Zone troops could withdraw 500 metres to the Main Line of Resistance where they could avoid the worst of the Allied artillery.

When a major Allied attack was imminent, German artillery would switch any predetermined fire from forward of the Outpost Line and direct it to fall on the Forward Zone itself, the German infantry given some 15 minutes to evacuate their previous positions. Once the main Allied barrage had begun, the German artillery would begin counter-battery fire in an attempt to disrupt the Allied bombardment. The main requirement for artillery was to deliver aimed fire onto the attacking Allied infantry and every attempt was made to provide German battalion and company sub-units with artillery observers and communications. Should Allied infantry penetrate the battalion positions, every opportunity would be taken to launch counter-attacks to regain the Forward Zone.

Within the Main Line of Resistance the objective was to create company positions with a series of interconnected trench lines, wire obstacles, light machine-guns and infantry guns designed to provide intimate support. The Main Line of Resistance would be some 300 to 400 metres in depth and was designed to lure attacking Allied infantry into terrain over which they would have had no prior observation. Disorientated, and under fire from a number of different directions, the attack would then break down. Behind the Main Line of Resistance would be a relatively empty space occupied by machine-gun posts which would become a rear battle zone, similar to the Main Line of Resistance.

Using the tactics outlined above, German doctrine sought to counteract Allied artillery superiority. In reality, the Germans found it increasingly difficult to deal with the Allied 'bite and hold' tactics which they termed 'small-scale attacks with limited objectives'. These attacks were too large to be dealt with by local battalion or regimental reserves and required dedicated counter-attack divisions to repulse the incursions. To be effective, these divisions needed to be deployed forward, but in doing so, they became vulnerable to Allied artillery, particularly when required to penetrate the Allied defensive barrage. This led to a reconsideration of tactics in late September 1917, with the decision made to reinforce the Forward Zone with troops from the counter-attack divisions to force Allied troops to hold their lines in greater strength and thus make them more vulnerable to German artillery.

The Battle of Broodseinde proved the error of reverting to a heavily defended forward line. With the best troops and weapons quickly neutralised or destroyed by Allied artillery fire in the Forward Zone, the German defence lost its coherence. Nor could the German reserves conduct effective counter-attacks, as the crisis in the Forward Zone saw them committed to defence in a piecemeal fashion. Thus on 7 October, just prior to the Passchendaele attack, Ludendorff rescinded the order to reinforce the Forward Zone and reverted to the main weight of the defence being conducted in the Main Line of Resistance. These late changes illustrate more than most the tactical dilemma that Allied artillery superiority imposed on the German Army. The Germans were forced into a cycle of constant tactical improvisation in what was ultimately an unsuccessful attempt to address their significant firepower and manpower deficiencies.

THE GERMAN 195TH INFANTRY DIVISION

The division responsible for the defence of Passchendaele on 12 October 1917 was the German Army's *195th Infantry Division*. Raised for service on the Eastern Front in July 1916, it took part in the Russian campaigns of late 1916. By 1917 the division comprised the *101st Reserve Infantry Brigade*, which had three infantry regiments, the *6th* and *8th Jager infantry regiments* and the *233rd Reserve Infantry Regiment*. In support of the infantry was a cavalry squadron (*3rd Squadron, 14th Uhlan Regiment*), a field artillery regiment (*200th Field Artillery Regiment*), a pioneer battalion, an ambulance company, two field hospitals and a motor transport column.

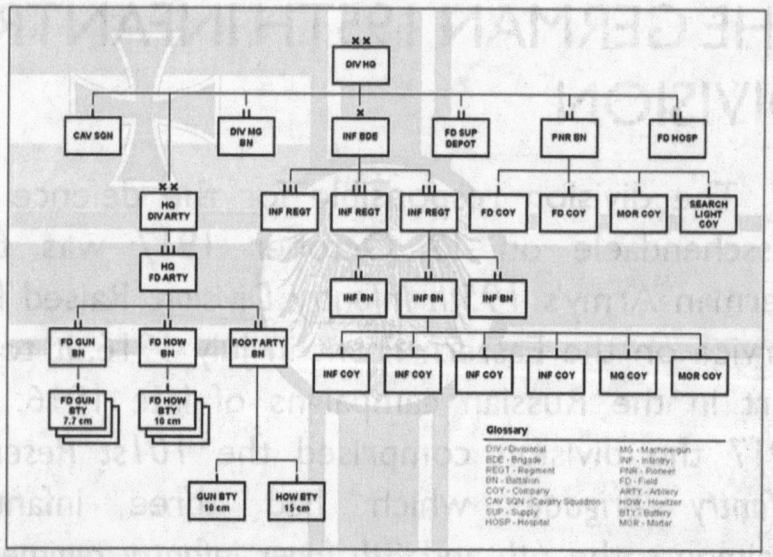

Diagram 4. The organisation of a German infantry division in 1917.

THE GERMAN 1908 PATTERN MACHINE-GUN AND 1908/15 PATTERN MACHINE-GUN

The German Army's principal medium machine-gun was the 1908 pattern machine-gun (MG 08). Based on the 1908 pattern Maxim design, it was a crew-served weapon that required four to six men to operate. The belt-fed, water-cooled gun was mounted on a heavy tripod or sled, which could be raised or lowered to ensure that the gun remained behind cover while firing. When mounted on its sled the machine-gun had an effective range of 2000 metres with a maximum rate of fire of 600 rounds per minute. It fired a .311-inch or 7.9mm bullet, which was the same calibre as the standard German infantry rifle, the 1898 pattern rifle the Gewehr 98 (Gew 98). The MG 08 fired a range of ammunition, including the standard lead bullet with steel jacket, a steel core armour-piercing round, a tracer round and an explosive round. While robust and reliable, the combined weight of the weapon and sled was 69kg, which increased with the additional weight of ammunition, water and protective shield. The basic machine-gun could only be carried around the battlefield by two soldiers using a special harness system which, while suitable for deploying guns to defensive positions, had obvious limitations when conducting attacks or counter-attacks. In order to meet the pressing tactical need for a light machine-gun, the German Army adapted the MG 08 by removing the heavy sled and adding a small bipod with a pistol grip and wooden stock. The weapon's weight was now reduced to 18kg and it could be carried by a single soldier with a sling. Ammunition could be either the original belted ammunition or a 100-round drum which was fitted to the gun. The new weapon was known as the 1908/1915 pattern light machine-gun (MG 08/15). While the removal of the heavy sled adversely affected stability and accuracy, the overall utility of the MG 08/15 over the MG 08 was amply demonstrated by the fact that, at the end of the war, a German infantry regiment had four times as many MG 08/15s (72 guns with six per infantry company) as MG 08s.

Located in a shell crater, this German MG 08 is mounted on a post, making it capable of all-round defence as well as anti-aircraft fire (AWM H13194).

A posed photograph of a German 1908/15 Pattern machine-gun team. The features which make the model deployable—the rifle-style stock, the drum magazine and the small bipod, are clearly visible (AWM C01089).

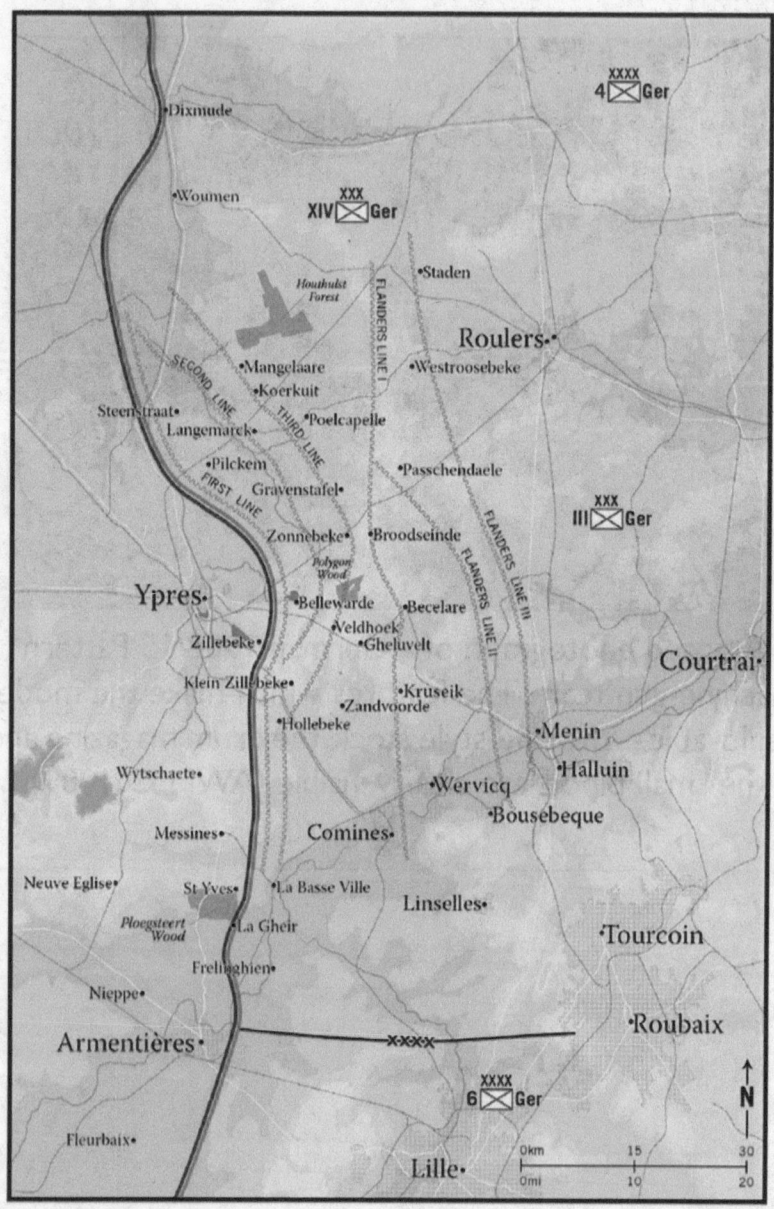

Map 6. The German defensive lines in Flanders in July 1917 prior to the commencement of the Third Ypres offensive. The defensive depth of the German position at Passchendaele, covered by Flanders Line I and Flanders Line II, is worthy of note.

The composition of the *195th Infantry Division* reflected the expedient nature of Falkenhayn's creation of new divisions. The two *Jäger* regiments were highly mobile light infantry designed to work in conjunction with German cavalry. However, by 1917 the opportunity for cavalry movement on the Western Front was extremely limited, so *Jäger* units were now deployed in more traditional infantry roles. In order to be effective in this new role, by 1916 the average *Jäger* battalion had a machine-gun company and a trench mortar company added to its order of battle. The third regiment in the division was a reserve regiment. In pre-war Germany, soldiers serving in reserve units would have had at least two years' regular army service with anything up to 28 years' reserve service. By 1917 manpower attrition was such that reserve units created in 1916 would only have four to five months' training before being committed to battle. Given that the average age of the division was 25, it was likely that the division's reserve infantry brigade had a mixture of older and younger reservists, giving it a broader experience base than a newly raised 1916 brigade. Despite the diverse nature of the original roles of the regiments within the division, culturally it was very homogenous, with all three regiments recruited from the *11th Corps* district around Kassel in western Germany.

The German defence lines before Passchendaele were known as the Flanders Line I and Flanders Line II and constituted the remnants of a defensive system that had been constructed to contain the BEF offensive following the Battle of Messines. Like other villages in the German defensive lines, the ruins of Passchendaele had been fortified with barbed wire and defensive posts in accordance with the principles of defence in depth. Nature provided an added layer of defence for the *195th Infantry Division*. The geology of Flanders consisted of topsoil on a clay base. This layer of clay ensured that any falls of heavy rain did not seep underground, but remained as surface water. The only way this surface water could be moved was through a network of streams, drainage canals and rivers. Once this network was destroyed by artillery fire, the surface water was no longer channelled away from the battlefield but pooled where it fell, creating bogs and swamps. South-west of Passchendaele, the destruction of the irrigation system had caused the Ravebeek and Stroombeek creeks to form a large swamp in the re-entrant leading up to the village, precluding the use of tanks and ensuring that infantry movement along this route would be very difficult.

However the clay soil did not act entirely in favour of the defender. When saturated with water the clay became plastic, causing trench walls to swell and collapse. Such conditions rendered the construction of any below-ground fortifications almost impossible and the Germans were forced to build defensive structures above ground, centred on pillboxes (or blockhouses) of reinforced concrete on the drier, upland areas around the village. Defenders outside these pillboxes sought protection from artillery fire and the weather in small lengths of trench with a roof of canvas or corrugated iron. Depending on the tactical situation, the German troops would then move between the pillboxes, trenches or water-filled shell holes. While the former were relatively easily identified, in the churned, featureless landscape that Flanders had become, any trench or shell hole that placed the soldier below the horizon offered reasonable concealment and protection.

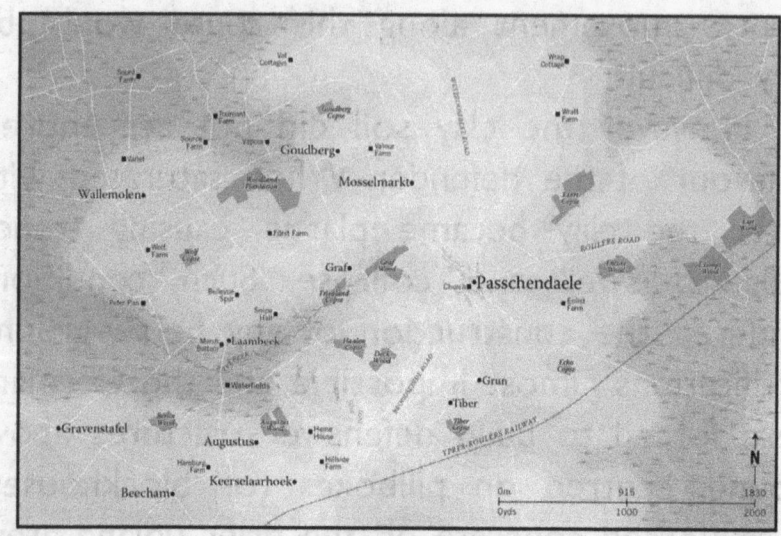

Map 7. Map outlining the wet and marshy areas around Passchendaele village in late October 1917. The relatively dry ground along Passchendaele Ridge (following the north-south Broodseinde-Passchendaele-Westroosebeke road) is evident, as is the dry ground leading back along the Bellevue spur to the Meetcheele and Mosselmarkt hamlets. The wet and swampy areas between Passchendaele Ridge and Bellevue spur have been formed by Ravebeek Creek which is flowing west into Stroombeek Creek.

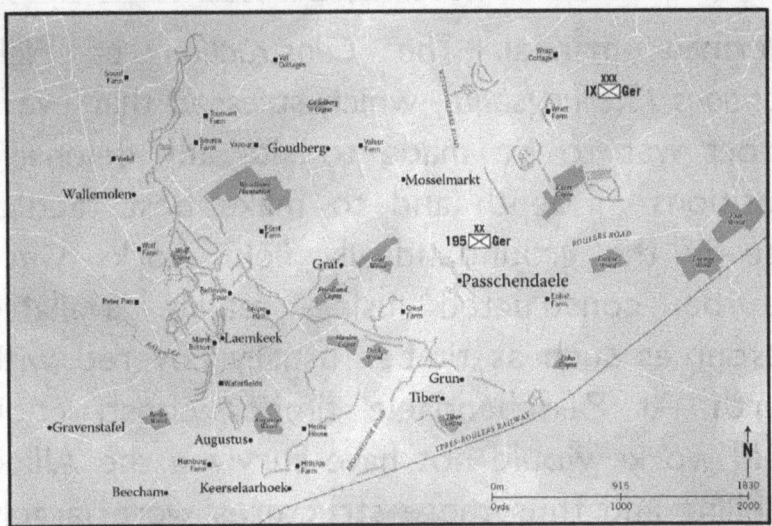

Map 8. Some of the identified German 195th Infantry Divisions barbed wire and defensive positions in the immediate surrounds of Passchendaele. This map is taken from the 1934 unit history of the 39th Battalion which appears to be based on the II ANZAC Corps Instruction Number 8 (Provisional) map.

PILLBOXES (OR BLOCKHOUSES)

While 'pillbox' was the commonly used Allied term for almost any substantial German defensive structure, in reality the German Army had a number of specialised designs for field works ranging from general accommodation dugouts, observations posts, machine-gun emplacements, headquarters dugouts, dugouts to hold reserves/reinforcements, and artillery emplacements. These fortification designs were generally standardised and covered in a 1916

German manual, *The Construction of Field Positions (Stellungsbau)*, which stressed that every effort was to be made to site any defensive positions in depth and to make best tactical use of the ground. Ideally, field works were to be constructed using readily available resources such as timber, usually covered with earth. At Passchendaele timber construction field works would not have survived the Allied shelling and thus these structures were largely built of concrete with a mixture of cement, sand and stone in the proportion of 1:2:4. To prevent any weakening of the pillbox, careful instructions were provided for the mixing and pouring of the concrete and, where possible, reinforcing rods of iron (typically railway tracks) were added to strengthen the structure. A thickness of 0.8 metres was regarded as sufficient to proof a wall against 6-inch guns, but special fieldworks, such as headquarters positions, received extra reinforcement to protect them from 8-inch shells. Walls of 0.4 metres could provide protection from splinters, but were not recommended since they did not provide full protection and often collapsed, with the resulting debris blocking any exits. To prevent the intrusion of poisonous gases, the entrances to structures were provided with a curtain that could be dampened with lime water. Swinging doors were not used as they could be blocked by falling earth. Because of the wet soil the majority of pillboxes at Passchendaele often had poor foundations, but were generally well sited and, when stoutly defended, posed a formidable obstacle.

Soldiers resting behind a German pillbox in the Ypres sector, 26 September 1917. The requirement to build above the high Flanders water table ensured that structures such as this stood out in the landscape (AWM E00898).

The division arrived in Ypres during May 1917 and was initially positioned in the Wytschaete sector, not arriving in Passchendaele until 3 October 1917. On 5 October, in response to the impending BEF attack at Poelcappelle, the *233rd Reserve Infantry Regiment* was ordered to take up a counter-attack position just to the east of Passchendaele. No sooner had it done so than, in accordance with German tactical doctrine, it came under command of the *20th Infantry Division* and was directed to relieve elements of German regiments already decimated by the BEF attack to the south-east of Passchendaele. Throughout 9 October, the regiment was subjected to the full force of Allied artillery fire and, as part of the *20th Infantry Division*, conducted a counter-attack to recapture those parts of the Passchendaele defence line that the British had recently overrun. The *233rd Reserve Infantry Regiment* was still holding these positions on the eve of 12 October. While this action was occurring, the rest of the *195th Infantry Division* had taken over the defence of Passchendaele from the *3rd Reserve Infantry Division*, with its two *Jager* regiments deployed to cover the approaches to the village. Thus, even before the Australian attack on 12 October, the regiments of the *195th Infantry Division* had seen their units battered in the defence of

Passchendaele as a result of the Poelcappelle attack on 9 October.

While Allied intelligence had a reasonably accurate picture of the capabilities of the *195th Infantry Division,* Monash's 'Notes of Operations of the 3rd Australian Division', written after the Passchendaele battle, apparently misidentifies the *8th Jager Regiment* as the *5th Jager Regiment.* Company strengths within the battalions of the *195th Infantry Division* were estimated to average 100 to 150 men, with reinforcements having been received prior to the battle from returned wounded and a small proportion of young recruits who would normally have been called up in 1919. Australian military intelligence also believed that the division had been equipped with an extra quota of light machine-guns, with the *233rd Reserve Infantry Regiment* possessing six light machine-guns per company. In this regard the Australian assessment was slightly awry since, as early as March 1917, the German Army had made six light machine-guns per company the standard to compensate for a reduction in the establishment strength of infantry companies. Overall, the Australian intelligence assessment of the *195th Infantry Division* was reasonably accurate and paints a picture of a capable division, an assessment that was reinforced by a post-war American military intelligence study of the

German Army. As such, the forthcoming battle between the 3rd Australian Division and the German *195th Infantry Division* was a relatively even match and the outcome would turn on factors such as planning and artillery rather than merely the quality of the troops involved.

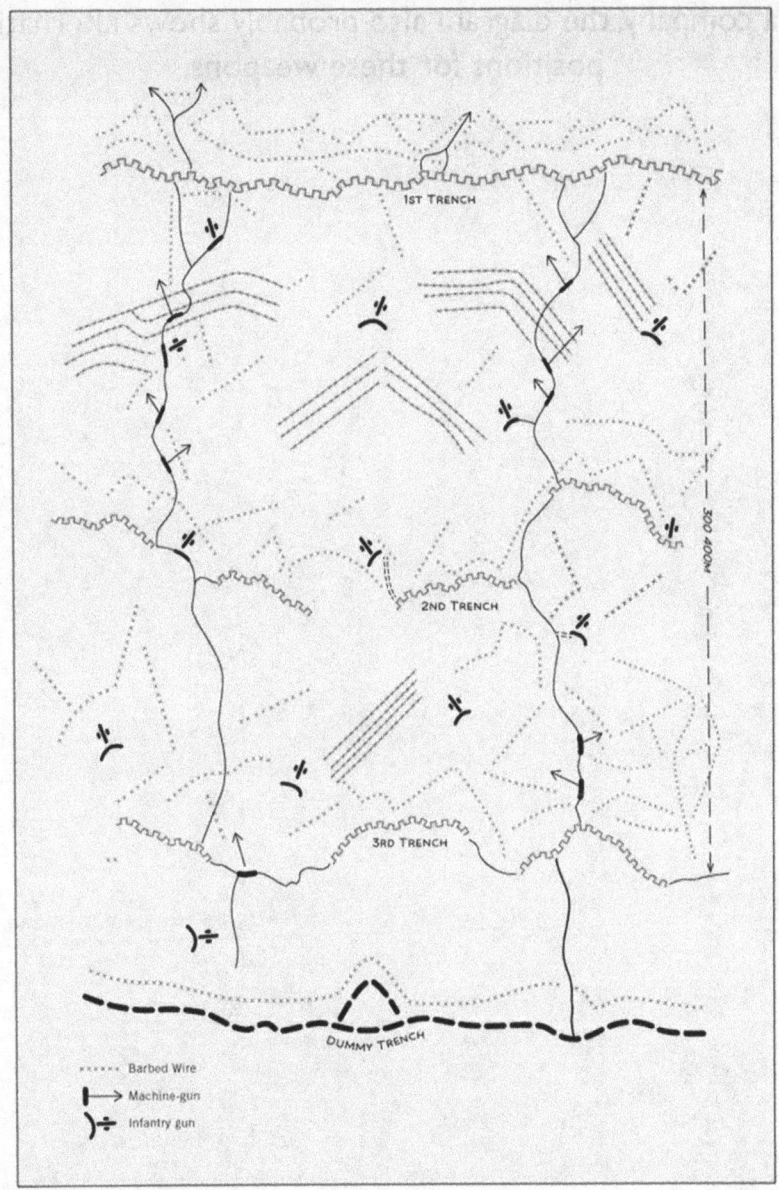

Diagram 5. A German Army diagram showing the 'Organisation of Company Sector for the Winter Months in the Wytschaete Group (IX Reserve Corps)', dated 5 September 1917. The symbols denote machine-guns and infantry guns. Given that the number of crew-served weapons on the diagram exceeds that normally allocated

to a company, the diagram also probably shows alternative positions for these weapons.

CHAPTER 4

PASSCHENDAELE I: PLANNING THE 3RD AUSTRALIAN DIVISION'S ATTACK

SECOND ARMY'S OUTLINE FOR THE ATTACK

The setback at Poelcappelle did not deter Haig from continuing the Ypres offensive. The strategic and operational-level considerations that led him to persist remained extant, despite the advent of near-constant rain from 4 October. Nevertheless, following the Poelcappelle battle, Plumer believed that the ground II ANZAC Corps had gained constituted an adequate jumping-off line for an attack on Passchendaele. There was also a belief in Plumer's Second Army Headquarters that the mud, rather than the German defences, was the primary reason for the failure of the Poelcappelle attack and hence another attack had every possibility of success.

In broad terms, Plumer saw the ensuing battle unfolding in a series of phases:

Phase One. II ANZAC Corps would capture the Passchendaele—Westroosebeke ridge in a single movement on 12 October.

Phase Two. II ANZAC Corps would be relieved by the Canadian Corps on 14 October.

Phase Three. The Canadian Corps would consolidate its Passchendaele position by advancing north-east towards Moorslede.

Phase Four. The Canadian Corps would relieve X Corps north of the Ypres—Menin road and, assisted by IX Corps, clear the rest of the German forces from the villages of Gheluvelt and Becelaere, south-east of Passchendaele.

The Second Army objective given to II ANZAC Corps was the same as that for the attack on 9 October—advance just beyond Passchendaele. To achieve this, the 3rd Australian Division and the New Zealand Division would relieve the 66th and 49th British divisions and launch the attack. The right flank of II ANZAC Corps would be secured by I ANZAC Corps with the 4th Australian Division and the left flank of II ANZAC Corps by the British XVIII Corps with the 9th Scottish Division.

II ANZAC CORPS PLANNING

The staff officers of Lieutenant General Godley's II ANZAC Corps quickly constructed a plan that conformed with Plumer's outline for the Passchendaele attack. By this stage of the war the corps and divisional planning process did not require a complete rewriting of planning fundamentals for each individual battle. Had this been the case, the ability of staff officers to produce detailed battle plans for corps-level attacks within such compressed time frames (4 October Broodseinde, 9 October Poelcappelle and 12 October Passchendaele) would have been limited. In drafting the Passchendaele battle orders and plan, the II ANZAC Corps staff relied heavily on previous planning guidance outlined in II ANZAC Corps' Instructions for the Offensive. These instructions were standardised procedures outlining the way II ANZAC Corps would fight its battles and were well understood by the officers and men who were to prosecute the attack. Without the requirement to rewrite the procedures for every attack in detail, the II ANZAC Corps staff officers could concentrate their planning attention on those features critical for the forthcoming attack. This also allowed those receiving the orders to understand the core aspects of a plan without being swamped by repetitive detail.

Following Poelcappelle, the 3rd Australian Division and the New Zealand Division, which were to lead the attack on Passchendaele, moved up to replace the 66th and 49th British divisions, currently occupying the front line. Corps-level instructions for this relief were issued on 8 October, with the move to occur on the night of 10/11 October. In a fine example of the level of interoperability that British and dominion divisions had achieved in the BEF, pioneer, engineer and medical units from the 66th and 49th British divisions remained in place. These units were taken under command by the incoming divisions (with the equivalent Australian and New Zealand units taken under command by the British divisions). The outgoing British divisions also continued to provide military police, traffic control, water point and ammunition parties for the incoming Australian and New Zealand divisions.

On 10 October, II ANZAC Corps received formal instructions from Plumer to recommence the offensive, issued as a II ANZAC Corps Instruction (although a provisional instruction had already been issued on 8 October). Plumer's outline for the attack had not been altered, and placed the 3rd Australian Division on the right and the New Zealand Division on the left. The corps attack would be divided into three objectives—Red Line (first objective), Blue Line (second objective) and Green Line (third objective)—with the Ypres—Roulers railway line (on the 3rd Australian Division's right flank) forming the boundary between I ANZAC Corps and II ANZAC Corps. The railway line was within I ANZAC Corps' allocated territory, which meant that the right forward brigade of the Australian division had an oblique, rather than a direct approach to the firmer ground of Passchendaele Ridge itself.

GENERAL SIR ALEXANDER JOHN GODLEY, CCB, KCMG

Born in England in 1867, Alexander Godley joined the British Army in 1886 and was commissioned into the Royal Dublin Infantry, subsequently serving in the Boer War. During the war he took part in the defence of Mafeking and also served on the staff of the then Lieutenant Colonel Herbert Plumer. In 1910 Godley was promoted to major general and given command of the New Zealand Territorial Force and, following the outbreak of war, the New Zealand Expeditionary Force. In Egypt Godley was appointed to command of the composite New Zealand and Australian Division for the Gallipoli campaign, assuming command of the ANZAC Corps from General Birdwood for the evacuation of the peninsula. In June 1916 he took II ANZAC Corps to France and remained its commander until January 1918 when it lost its Australian divisions and was retitled XXII Corps. The New Zealand Division's heavy losses at Passchendaele saw Godley's reputation with the New Zealand public suffer, but the government stood by him and he led the New Zealand Expeditionary Force for the remainder of the conflict. Following the Armistice, Godley served as Military Secretary to the Secretary of State for War from 1920 to 1922 before commanding the British Army on the Rhine from 1922 to 1924. After serving as GOC Southern Command from 1924 to 1928, he was Governor of Gibraltar until his retirement in 1933. Following the outbreak of the Second World War Godley commanded a platoon in the Home Guard. He died at Oxford in 1957 aged 90.

Post-war portrait of General Sir Alexander Godley (AWM P03717.003).

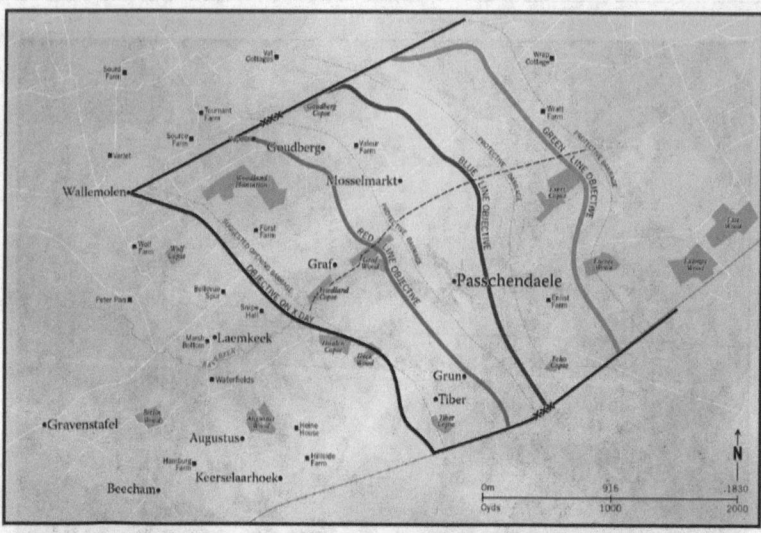

Map 9. The original map dated 9 October 1917 showing the three stages and objectives for the attack (Red, Blue and Green lines), corps boundaries and the proposed artillery barrage lines.

AUSTRALIAN ARTILLERY: ORDNANCE QF 18-POUNDER AND ORDNANCE QF 4.5-INCH HOWITZER

By the outbreak of war the British Army had equipped its infantry divisions with three artillery pieces, the Ordnance QF 18-pounder, the Ordnance QF 4.5-inch howitzer and the Ordnance BL 60-pounder. QF stood for 'quick firing', denoting a gun that had a single-piece metal cartridge case for its shell and a recoil system which kept the gun carriage steady while the gun was being fired. These two innovations meant that gunners could maintain a rapid rate of fire onto a target without the requirement to constantly readjust the sights. The early Mk I and II QF 18-pounder fired an 8.4kg (18.5lb) shell of 83.8mm (3.3-inch) calibre to an effective range of 5900 metres with a sustained rate of fire of 4 rpm. The Mk I and II QF 4.5-inch howitzer fired a 16kg (35lb) shell of 114mm (4.5-inch) calibre to a maximum range of 6700 metres with a rate of fire also at 4 rpm. The two weapons were complementary, the QF 18-pounder boasting a flat trajectory for line of sight targets, while the QF 4.5-inch howitzer fired at a high angle, its shell searching out targets behind cover and in trenches. The Mk I and II BL 60-pounder fired a 27kg (60lb) shell of 127mm (5-inch) calibre to a maximum range of 14,200 metres at a rate of 2 rpm. The BL 60-pounder was primarily used for counter-battery fire. In 1914 each BEF infantry division had three field artillery brigades of 18-pounders, one brigade of 4.5-inch howitzers and a battery of 60-pounders, all commanded by a brigadier general with the title of Commander Royal Artillery. While Australian infantry divisions were initially deployed with only 18-pounders (relying on British heavy artillery), by 1917 the war establishment of an Australian infantry division included two field artillery brigades, each with three 18-pounder batteries and one 4.5-inch howitzer battery. The Australian divisions continued to rely on BEF heavy artillery, but experience dictated a growth in trench mortars with each Australian field artillery brigade now equipped with three trench mortar batteries and one heavy trench mortar battery.

An Australian 18-pounder battery at Ypres in 1917. The stockpile of shells provides some indication of the rate of fire required to sustain a barrage (AWM E00920).

An Australian gunner from the 11th Field Battery standing next to his dug-in and camouflaged 4.5-inch howitzer at Ypres (AWM C04390).

The artillery barrage was planned along the same lines as previous attacks conducted under Plumer's 'bite and hold' doctrine. It would consist of five waves (A, B, C, D and E) fired by the following weapons:

    Wave A: 18-pounder field guns
    Wave B: 4.5-inch howitzers and 18-pounders
    Wave C: machine-guns
    Wave D: 8-inch howitzers
    Wave E: 8-inch howitzers, 9.2-inch howitzers and 60-pounders

These wave barrages would be fired in sequences, the order of these sequences determined by how close the advancing troops could safely move behind the appropriate barrage. Corps orders stressed that the attacking troops should thoroughly understand the nature of the barrage and how closely the advance could follow the wave barrage being fired. In a further safety measure, the starting line for the infantry attack would be at least 119 metres from the initial barrage line, but no further than this, to allow the infantry to close up to the barrage before it lifted.

The artillery barrage would open fire at zero hour with a rate of fire of two rounds per gun per minute. This rate of fire would rise to four rounds per gun per minute at zero hour plus eight minutes. After this, the barrage would maintain a uniform rate of fire, advancing 91 metres (100 yards) every eight minutes firing at a rate of two rounds per gun per minute. The barrage would then halt on the Red and Blue protective barrage lines, to allow the infantry to catch up. The Green protective barrage line would be fired if the corps advance captured Passchendaele and exploited the area immediately beyond it. At the protective barrage lines, the rate of fire would be reduced to one round per gun per minute. While the barrages were advancing with the infantry, approximately 30% of the heavy artillery allocated for the attack would bombard individual strongpoints, dugouts and houses in and around Passchendaele from zero hour on. Such targeting would be based on photos provided by aerial reconnaissance from No.21 Squadron, Royal Flying Corps, flying in support of II ANZAC Corps. While such detailed artillery planning was standard for any battle, latitude was also given to the commander of the II ANZAC Corps artillery to reduce the rate of fire used in previous attacks, should there be insufficient time to replenish munitions dumps before the attack on Passchendaele.

The use of a machine-gun barrage saw medium machine-guns (the Vickers Mk I) collected in company-sized groupings to provide indirect fire onto the German lines. Special attention was paid to the employment of the machine-gun in barrage planning. Experience had shown that a machine-gun barrage acted as a strong indicator to the defending Germans that an attack was to be launched and that the shelling they were enduring was not just a practice barrage. For this reason, the machine-gun barrage would not open fire until zero hour plus three minutes. It would fire for two minutes on its opening line at double the normal rate of fire, before dropping to a normal rate of fire.

Corps Headquarters would determine the rate of advance for the attack using flares fired by the forward troops at zero plus two hours and 30 minutes, zero plus four hours and 30 minutes and zero plus seven hours. The position of these flares would be noted by an aircraft flying overhead. The aircrew would mark the extent of the corps advance on a map, which would then be dropped at II ANZAC Corps Headquarters. In a further control measure, when each barrage reached a halt line (such as a Red or Blue protective barrage line), each 18-pounder battery would fire smoke shells for a period of five minutes to signal to the infantry the rate at which the barrage would advance.

3RD AUSTRALIAN DIVISION PLANNING

Monash submitted a broad outline of his divisional plan in writing to Godley's headquarters on 9 October. As expected, this followed the requirements outlined in the II ANZAC Corps plan, but such acquiescence was not an automatic requirement of the BEF planning process. It was not unusual for plans to be adjusted at army or corps-level planning conferences or through personal correspondence between divisional and corps commanders. Due to the scale of forces involved, planning at army and corps-level headquarters was by its very nature more conceptual and less detailed than the planning conducted at the division or brigade level. It was at this lower level that Monash operated and, as such, his planning would have greater relevance for his brigades and battalions during the conduct of the forthcoming battle.

The plan Monash submitted to Godley on 9 October had two brigades leading the attack with a third in reserve. The two attacking brigades would lead with a battalion frontage only, the plan calling for the leading battalion to capture the first objective (Red Line), the next battalion to pass through the Red Line and capture the second objective (Blue Line), and the third battalion to pass through the secured Red and Blue lines and capture the Green Line. Each attacking brigade was to have a battalion in reserve. The left-hand brigade (10th Brigade) would advance through Passchendaele, with the battalion tasked to capture the village (the 38th Battalion) reinforced by a company from the 39th Battalion.

Should the left-hand brigade (10th Brigade) became bogged down in Passchendaele, the New Zealand Division would assist with mopping-up operations within the village. The reserve battalion from the 9th Brigade would also be allocated to assist the 10th Brigade should it be unable to secure its third objective (the Green Line) to prevent a gap opening between the 9th Brigade and the New Zealand Division. Once the three objectives were secured, the division would dig two continuous lines on the Blue and Green lines in preparation for the expected German counter-attack. Of the indirect fire assets still under divisional control, Monash directed that all Vickers machine-guns (less 16) be employed in the machine-gun barrage. Eight Vickers machine-guns would be left under control of each of the two attacking brigades to be deployed as they saw fit. Each brigade was allocated six Stokes mortars during the advance and would hold two in reserve.

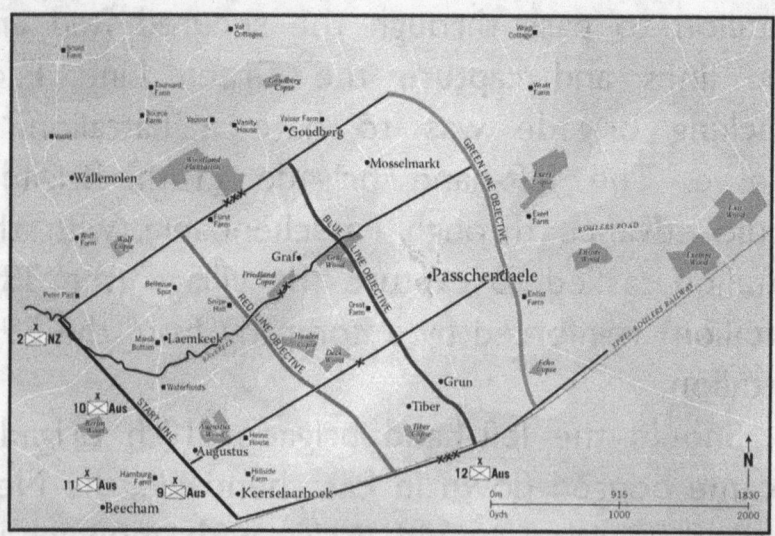

Map 10. Location of the 3rd Australian Division and flanking brigades on 12 October 1917, prior to the attack. On the left flank, the divisional boundary between the 3rd

Australian Division and the New Zealand Division follows Ravebeek Creek. On the right flank, the boundary between the 3rd and 4th Australian divisions is the Ypres—Roulers railway line. Within the 3rd Australian Division area, the 10th Brigade is on the left and tasked with capturing Passchendaele, with the 9th Brigade in support on its right. The 11th Brigade is in reserve and holding the line to the rear of the 10th and 9th brigades.

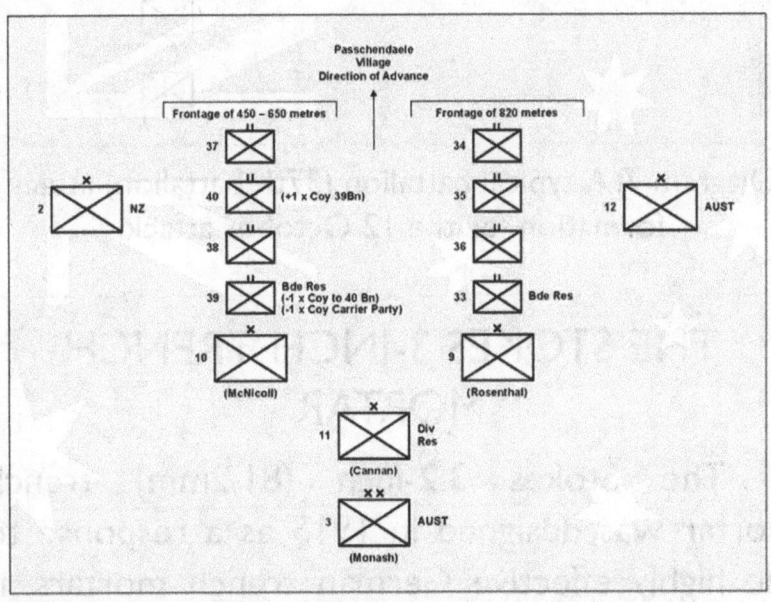

Diagram 6. The 3rd Australian Division's brigade and battalion attack formations for the 12 October attack.

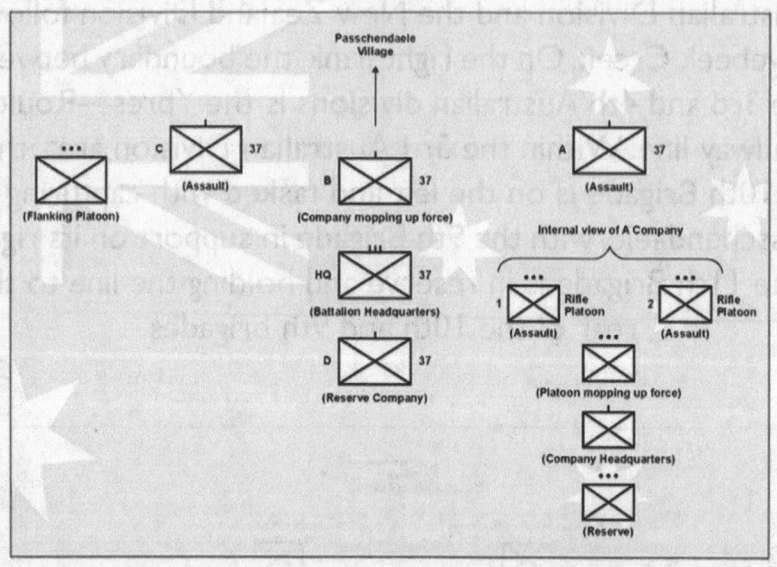

Diagram 7. A typical battalion (37th Battalion) attack formation for the 12 October attack.

THE STOKES 3-INCH TRENCH MORTAR

The Stokes 3.2-inch (81.2mm) trench mortar was designed in 1915 as a response to the highly effective German trench mortars. It was a simple weapon consisting of a steel tube, base plate, and bipod. The mortar bomb was dropped down the tube where it struck a stud at the end of the breech piece, firing the bomb. The mortar was capable of being broken down into three individual loads (mortar tube 22kg, bipod stand 15kg and base plate 27kg) and moved by two to three men around the battlefield. This compared very favourably with the German 7.6cm (light) *minenwerfer* which weighed 140kg and was generally moved by horse and cart. However the Stokes mortar's rapid rate of fire (6 to 8 rpm at a sustainable rate or 25 rpm at a maximum rate) meant that, during an attack, additional soldiers would have to accompany the weapon to keep it supplied with bombs. With a box of three mortar rounds (including fuses, detonator and cartridges) weighing up to 20kg, keeping the mortar supplied and firing at the sustainable rate required considerable logistic effort. To assist the soldiers, a dedicated canvas carrying harness was designed in the form of a sleeveless jacket with pockets to carry four bombs and their individual fuses. The mortar fired high explosive bombs to a maximum range of 730 metres, with a minimum range of 90 metres. By 1919 an armoured shield had been designed for the mortar, but with a weight of 122kg, this could only have been used in static positions. According to the *1919 Handbook of the M.L. Stokes 3-inch trench Mortar Equipments*, an anti-aircraft mount with mirror sight was also provided for the weapon, although determining how this would actually work in practice requires some imagination.

Australian soldiers receive instruction in the use of the Stokes trench mortar at La Houssoye, France, December 1916 (AWM E00066).

On receiving his plan, II ANZAC Corps Headquarters rang Monash to discuss its details. In particular, the headquarters was concerned about three issues: the allocation of insufficient troops to the first wave of the Australian attack which comprised a single battalion from each brigade; the bombardment plan for the German positions in the Forward Zone, which was considered too light; and the depth of penetration for the Australian attack which was considered too shallow. Monash responded by letter on 10 October. He defended his decision to have each brigade attack spearheaded by a single battalion by arguing that a battalion frontage was a natural outcome of the corps plan allocated to his division. Further, Monash felt that, with the forces available, he could attack with a battalion frontage of 450 to 550 metres with a density of one man for every metre. In the tactical mathematics of the period, Monash reasoned that such a troop density would be sufficient to overcome the German *195th Division* since it was holding its forward positions with just a battalion—a density of no more than one man every three metres. This gave the attacking Australian battalions a 3:1 advantage in men per metre and, when combined with the advancing barrage, Monash considered this numerical advantage adequate to win the battle.

In responding to criticism of the bombardment plan, Monash argued that the strength of the artillery bombardment of the German Forward Zone was entirely dependent on the width of no man's land. If heavy artillery was to bombard German strongpoints 275 to 365 metres from the Australian lines, his troops would have to be withdrawn to a safe distance. Such a withdrawal would be difficult to accomplish as it was likely to occur at night. Far better, Monash asserted, to rely on more numerous practice barrages than the destructive capacity of heavy barrages to break the enemy's morale. Like the Broodseinde attack, Monash's preference was to have the initial bombardment within 137 metres of the Australian side of the Germans' closest forward position, with the Australian troops withdrawing to a safe distance some 30 minutes prior to zero hour.

On the final point raised by II ANZAC Corps Headquarters, that of the possibility of deeper penetration and exploitation of the German line, Monash considered the Green Line to be at the extreme limit of the divisional artillery. He believed it to be unwise to proceed beyond effective artillery support because of the risk of determined German counter-attacks overwhelming the Australian troops who, by then, would be exhausted.

On the eve of the battle, Plumer's Chief of Staff, Major General Harington, wrote to Monash extending his best wishes for the forthcoming battle. In the patriotic prose of the time he told Monash:

> ...directly that you report it [the flag] is flying over Passchendaele it will be wired to England and Australia and that the C in C [Haig] knows well that once it is put up nothing will bring it down again.

Harington expressed concern over Monash's right flank and added a special reference to Second Army orders describing the junction point between I ANZAC Corps and II ANZAC Corps on the Ypres—Roulers railway line. He also spoke to Birdwood to ensure that I ANZAC Corps would advance simultaneously with II ANZAC Corps to protect Monash's right flank. Harington instructed that I ANZAC Corps should seize or dominate high ground north of Broubeek to prevent German interference with the right flank of the 3rd Australian Division.

Monash's detailed plan for the attack was released to his division on 9 October 1917 as Ypres Battle General Staff Circular Number 26. Amendments to the plan (Nos 27 and 28) were released on 10 October and again on 11 October (Nos 29 and 30). In an indication of the flexibility of the planning process, the day of the attack (12 October) and zero hour (5.25am) were not formally confirmed until 11 October.

The building used as the 3rd Australian Division Headquarters during the battles of Broodseinde and Passchendaele (to the left of the ambulance). The last of the division's brigades had left the Ypres area on 22 October and it is doubtful whether the soldiers in this photograph are from the 3rd Australian Division (AWM E01184).

BRIGADE PLANNING

Headquarters staff officers from the three Australian brigades had closely followed the progress of the 66th and 49th British divisions during the Poelcappelle attack. By the afternoon of 9 October the commander of the 9th Brigade (Brigadier General Rosenthal) and his key staff were already undertaking a reconnaissance of the positions held by the 66th British Division for the planned divisional relief. The commanders and staff of the 10th Brigade (Brigadier General McNicoll) and 11th Brigade (Brigadier General Cannan) conducted similar activities. Later that night the Brigade Majors (the key operational planning officers for a brigade) were summoned to Monash's headquarters to receive his outline plan for the attack. Amendments to this plan were delivered verbally to all brigade staff officers by Monash's divisional staff as late as 1.00pm on 10 October, with the details for the start line for the attack and H Hour not released until 2.30pm on 11 October. That evening the Brigade Majors, assisted by sapper officers, pegged out the battalion start lines which were then checked by the officers of the attacking battalions.

MAJOR GENERAL SIR CHARLES ROSENTHAL, KCB, CMG, DSO, VD

Born in Berrima in 1875, Charles Rosenthal was the son of Scandinavian migrants. He trained as an architect and practised his profession in Victoria, New South Wales and Western Australia. He joined the Geelong Battery of the Victoria Militia Garrison Artillery in 1892, was commissioned in 1903 and transferred to the Australian Field Artillery in 1908, commanding a battery. In 1914 he was given command of the 5th Field Artillery Brigade before transferring to the AIF and command of the 3rd Field Artillery Brigade. He was twice wounded at Gallipoli, the second wound requiring evacuation to England. When he returned to Egypt he was promoted to brigadier general and given command of the 4th Australian Division artillery. Serving through the Somme campaign, Rosenthal was wounded for a third time in 1916. In July 1917 he was appointed commander of the 9th Brigade, leading his men through the Third Ypres campaign. In May 1918 he was promoted to major general and assumed command of the 2nd Australian Division before being wounded for a fourth time during the Battle of Hamel. He had recovered sufficiently by August to lead his division though the remainder of the war, including the capture of Montbrehain, the last Australian action of the conflict. In 1919 Rosenthal supervised the AIF personnel depots during the repatriation of the force to Australia. Returning to Australia in 1920 he resumed his architectural practice and remained in the militia, commanding the 2nd Australian Division from 1921 to 1926 and again from 1932 to 1937. He served in the New South Wales Parliament between 1922 and 1925 and between 1936 and 1937, founding the King and Empire Alliance in 1921. He was twice President of the Institute of Architects of New South Wales and also President of the Australian Institute of Architects. From 1937 to 1945 he was the Administrator of Norfolk Island. He died in 1954 at Green Point, New South Wales, aged 79.

Portrait of Charles Rosenthal following his promotion to major general in May 1918 (AWM H19207).

THE 9TH BRIGADE PLAN

The plan for the 9th Brigade naturally followed that of the division. However, the post-action report on the attack made the magnitude of the task facing the brigade evident:

> It had been intended that the attack on the 12-10-17 should be made from the final objective set down for the attack by the 66th Division on 9-10-17, but as this attack gained practically no territory it was decided by higher authority that the attack on 12-10-17 should include the ground which had been set for the 66th Division and which they had failed to capture, plus the ground originally intended for the attack on 12-10-17. This meant an attack to a depth of 2500 yards on the right and 2600 yards on the left, over ground which was shell torn [and] very wet and muddy.

Because its right flank was on the Ypres—Roulers railway line, the frontage to be covered by the brigade increased from 731 metres at the start line to 822 metres by the final objective. While not a large increase, this 'expanding funnel' effect meant that the numerical superiority the Australians enjoyed over the defending Germans decreased the further the attack progressed from the start line.

The battalion tasks were those allocated by the divisional staff:

34th Battalion to capture the RED Line.

35th Battalion to capture the BLUE Line—less one company which was allocated the task of assisting the 10th Brigade attack on Passchendaele by a flank attack from the south.

36th Battalion to capture the GREEN Line.

33rd Battalion held as the Brigade Reserve.

Divisional orders permitted 16 Vickers machine-guns to remain within the brigades, while each of the attacking battalions had a detachment of two Vickers guns from the 9th Australian Machine Gun Company. Two Stokes mortars of the 9th Australian Light Trench Mortar Battery were also allocated to each battalion. The three assaulting battalions were to attack on a three-company frontage with a company in reserve. Each company was to have a three-platoon frontage with one platoon in reserve. Special parties were detailed to move on the flank of each battalion to ensure that contact was maintained with flanking units. At the start line, all three assembled battalions were to have a depth no greater than 91 metres. This would ensure they quickly cleared the German barrage line immediately after the attack commenced.

THE 10TH BRIGADE PLAN

Like the 9th Brigade, the 10th Brigade plan would also adhere closely to divisional orders. While the battalions of the 10th Brigade would have the same Red, Blue and Green Line objectives, these were described in terms of the brigade's specific area and as they appeared on the brigade map:

> 40th Battalion to capture and mop up all territory in area A.B. to C.D. (RED Line).
>
> 38th Battalion plus one company of the 39th Battalion to capture and mop up all territory from C.D. to E.F. (BLUE Line).
>
> 37th Battalion to capture and mop up all territory from E.F. to G.H. (GREEN Line).
>
> 39th Battalion (less two companies) to be the Brigade Reserve.

Of the two companies detached from the 39th Battalion, one was attached to the 38th Battalion and one allocated to brigade carrying parties. Among other tasks, these carrying parties would transport ammunition forward to the attacking battalions.

The battalion assault formation described above was issued as the 'Tenth Australian Infantry Brigade Order Number 68' on 9 October. On 10 October an Appendix (Appendix F) to Order Number 68 was issued. Marked SECRET and URGENT, this order conveyed a significant change. The brigade limit of advance was now reduced to the brigade line E.F. (the divisional Blue Line) not the divisional Green Line and a new objective would also be inserted, that of the start line to objective A.B. The decision to reduce the limit of the advance and insert a new objective saw the battalion objectives revised as follows:

> 37th Battalion to capture the first objective from the jump off line [start line] up to the brigade line A.B. [the divisional Red Line].
>
> The objective of the 40th Battalion will be practically the same as at present [The objective was to remain unchanged in securing A.B. to C.D., except that the divisional Red Line had now became the brigade Blue Line].
>
> The objective of the 38th Battalion will be practically the same as at present [to capture and mop up all territory from C.D. to E.F.—the divisional Blue Line that had now become the brigade Green Line].

39th Battalion (less two companies) remains the Brigade Reserve.

The potential for confusion caused by this late change is self-evident (indeed Bean in the *Official History* still lists the order of assault as the 37th, 38th, and 40th battalions respectively). While the reason for the change is not given in Appendix F, it could only have been as a result of the ill-defined start line caused by the failure of the earlier Poelcappelle attack. The problem this caused the 10th Brigade was spelt out in the 40th Battalion history:

> The only thing that was not clear was the line from which the attack by the 10th Brigade would be launched. This obscurity was the result of the failure of the attack by the 66th Division. The position was not clear, and very little information could be obtained. The proposed jumping-off line for the 12th October was changed repeatedly as the information varied.

BRIGADIER GENERAL SIR WALTER RAMSEY MCNICOLL, KBE, CB, CMG, DSO, VD

Born in Melbourne in 1877, Walter McNicoll was educated at state schools. He joined the Victorian Education Department in

1893, becoming a pupil-teacher in 1895, and obtained his Trained Teacher's Certificate in 1901. In 1905 he was on the staff of the newly opened Melbourne Continuation (High) School where he commanded the cadets. By 1911 he was founding headmaster of the future Geelong High School and a major in the militia. With the raising of the AIF, McNicoll was appointed second-in-command of the 7th Battalion and in April 1915 given command of the 6th Battalion. He was severely wounded at Gallipoli and, after an operation in London, was repatriated to Australia in late 1915. In February 1916 he was given command of the newly raised 10th Brigade, rejoining his men in England and leading the brigade through the Third Ypres campaign. When Monash was appointed corps commander, he favoured McNicoll as his replacement to command the 3rd Australian Division, but the appointment went to Brigadier General Gellibrand. McNicoll led the 10th Brigade through the remainder of the war and, following the Armistice, was appointed Inspector-General of Education, providing civilian education programs to soldiers waiting to return to Australia. Arriving back in Australia in late 1919, McNicoll resumed teaching and became Principal of the

Presbyterian Ladies' College at Goulburn. In 1931 he entered federal politics and won the seat of Werriwa for the Country Party. Leaving politics in 1934 he was appointed Administrator of the Mandated Territory of New' Guinea, a post he held on the outbreak of war in 1939. With the increasing likelihood of a Japanese invasion, McNicoll pressed the government for reinforcements to protect the Territory but was unsuccessful. Following the Japanese invasion in 1942 McNicoll was evacuated south, suffering from malaria. He retired as Administrator in 1942 and died in Sydney in 1947.

Brigadier General McNicoll sitting with his captured German messenger dog, Karl, outside his brigade headquarters at Heilly, northern France, 5 April 1918 (AWM E04699).

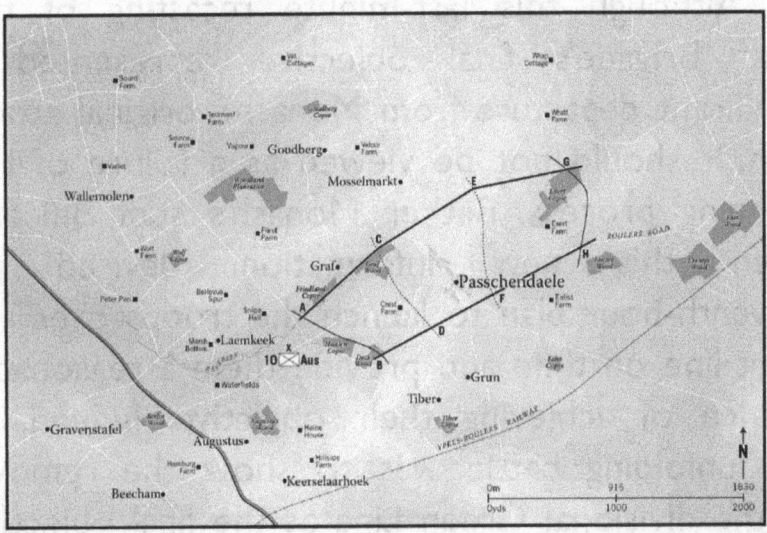

Map 11. Original map dated 9 October 1917 and showing the 10th Brigade boundary and the alphabetical areas each battalion in the brigade was responsible for clearing during the Passchendaele attack.

It was not until the 11th Brigade relieved the 66th British Division on 11 October that the actual location of the front line was determined. This saw the start line moved back to the limit of the advance that the 10th Brigade had achieved on 4 October, recognition that the 10th Brigade had to secure more ground during the initial phase of the attack (to the Red Line) than the divisional plan envisaged. As such, the hoped-for limit of the brigade advance to the divisional Green Line was no longer possible and the furthest the 10th Brigade could advance was to the brigade line E.F.

Although this last-minute recasting of the 10th Brigade's final objective represented a significant departure from Monash's original attack plan, it should not be viewed as a failure of the planning process. Rather Monash's staff officers, given this new information, devised an eleventh-hour plan to launch the troops over the start line on time and provide them a reasonable chance of achieving their objective. Indeed, as the unfolding battle was to show, the removal of the divisional Green Line as the final objective for the 10th Brigade would have little significance. A more important consequence was the increase in speed required of the advancing barrage which, due to the increased distance to be covered, was now allocated just 20 minutes to cover the initial 450 metres of the brigade advance instead of the planned 40. Given no increase in the number or rate of guns firing on a target, this resulted in a 'thinner' barrage for the attacking troops since the time the barrage spent on any specific target was now theoretically reduced by half.

While the battalion objectives were adjusted in Appendix F, the battalion groupings were not, since this would have produced significant disruption at the company level. Unlike the 9th Brigade, which allocated its indirect fire assets uniformly throughout the battalions, the 10th Brigade awarded a preponderance of firepower to the battalion tasked with the capture of the village. Thus the 38th Battalion was allocated four Vickers machine-gun teams and six Stokes mortars. The headquarters of the 10th Light Trench Mortar Battery also moved with the 38th Battalion, giving the Commanding Officer of the 38th the benefit of specialised staff to employ the Stokes mortars. Once Passchendaele was captured, the 10th Light Trench Mortar Battery would advance and support the 37th Battalion. The two remaining brigade Vickers machine-guns were allocated to the 39th Battalion as part of the Brigade Reserve.

THE 11TH BRIGADE PLAN

Allocated as the Brigade Reserve for the attack, the 11th Brigade's primary task was to occupy the front line previously held by the 66th British Division immediately before the attack and, in doing so, provide a secure base for the other two attacking brigades. Once the attack commenced, the 11th Brigade would stand ready to be deployed as 3rd Division Headquarters saw fit. If not directly deployed by Monash in the attack as a Divisional Reserve, the 11th Brigade would then relieve the now spent 9th and 10th brigades and hold the new front line following the battle until the entire division was relieved.

MAJOR GENERAL JAMES HAROLD CANNAN, CB, CMG, DSO, VD

Born in Townsville in 1882, James Cannan was educated at Brisbane Central Boys' School and Brisbane Grammar. He worked in the hardware industry before moving into insurance in 1910. In 1903 he was commissioned into the 1st Queensland (Moreton) Regiment and in 1912 transferred to the 8th Infantry (Oxley) Battalion. In 1914 he joined the AIF and took command of the 15th Battalion, leading it during the Gallipoli campaign before being invalided to England in October 1915. Returning to command of the 15th Battalion, he led the unit during the fighting at Pozières and Mouquet Farm and was promoted to brigadier general in August 1916 with command of the 11th Brigade. Cannan led his brigade through Third Ypres and the subsequent battles. He publicly clashed with Monash on at least one occasion, accusing him of favouritism towards the 10th Brigade. Following the Armistice,

Cannan studied insurance practices in London before returning to Australia in 1919 and discharging from the AIF. He resumed his career in the insurance industry and became Queensland President of the Returned Sailors and Soldiers Imperial League of Australia from 1920 to 1921 and Brisbane Legacy's first president in 1928. He returned to the militia and commanded the 2nd and 11th (Mixed) brigades before transferring to the Unattached List in 1925. In July 1940 he was recalled to active service, promoted to major general and given command of the 2nd Australian Division. In October 1940 he was made Quartermaster General and appointed to the Military Board. Responsible for logistic services in the South-West Pacific Area, he worked closely with General Blamey throughout the latter years of the Pacific War. In 1946 Cannan retired from the insurance industry and the militia, becoming Director, South-West Pacific Area, United Nations Relief and Rehabilitation Administration (1946-47), the Queensland Division of the Australian Red Cross Society (1950-51) and the Services Canteen Trust (1948-57). He died in Brisbane in 1976.

A 1944 portrait of Major General James Cannan as Quartermaster General, Land Headquarters (AWM 107663).

CHAPTER 5

PASSCHENDAELE I: THE 3RD AUSTRALIAN DIVISION'S ATTACK

On 10 October the 9th and 10th brigades spent the night in the line, spread throughout a series of fields east and south-east of Ypres. The allocated tents had not arrived, so the troops made do with whatever shelter they could improvise. By 6.00pm the next evening the brigades had commenced their move from their assembly areas behind Pilckem Ridge to their respective start lines. Light showers had fallen throughout the day and resumed at 1.30am. By 3.30am these showers had developed into heavy rain. Gough made a last-minute attempt to delay the attack, calling Plumer that night seeking a postponement given his concerns over the impact of the weather on supporting attacks by Fifth Army. In his memoirs, Gough writes that Plumer did not immediately reply to his request, indicating that he would seek the opinions of his corps commanders. Shortly after 8.00pm Plumer rang Gough to tell him that his corps commanders had advised that the attack should proceed, giving Gough no choice but to continue with his supporting attack.

THE APPROACH MARCH

The two brigades followed individual approach routes to their respective start lines, both of which led off the Zonnebeke Road. This road had been heavily bombed by the Germans and was in a terrible condition, a member of the 37th Battalion remarking that 'Capsized and bogged guns, smashed lorries and ammunition limbers, dead mules and horses, and dead men lined the Zonnebeke and Menin Road for miles.'

After leaving the Zonnebeke Road the 10th Brigade moved along 'K' Track, which consisted of a double row of duckboards leading to the forming-up point just behind the brigade start line. Progress along this duckboard track was slow due to the darkness, intermittent shelling and troop congestion. A constant pageant of German flares also halted troop movement, as soldiers froze to avoid betraying their position to German observers, resulting in much muttering and cursing as the concertina effect of the stop-start process worked its way down 'K' Track. German shelling had destroyed many of the duckboards, forcing the troops to walk around the splintered sections and step into the mud, which could be up to a metre deep. Once back on the duckboards, the mixture of mud, boots and rain ensured the undamaged boards became extremely slippery, causing soldiers to slip off into the mire.

A wrecked wagon on the Ypres—Zonnebeke road in early October illustrates both the state of the road and the dangers posed by German artillery (AWM E00951).

The track terminated in a sunken road just to the rear of the brigade start line where a party of soldiers and engineers from the 37th Battalion had placed the white tape for the battalion assembly point. The engineers had moved across to the right to continue the process for the 9th Brigade. In the immediate area of the 37th Battalion start line, dead and wounded British soldiers from the Poelcappelle attack still lay on the battlefield. The wounded pleaded for assistance but, given the pending attack, the infantry could not spare the manpower required to carry them to the rear, so they were left where they had fallen.

The 40th Battalion was the next to move into position, huddling up along a road parallel to an entrenchment named Dab Trench. With little room, the battalion's disposition was cramped, the plan for the men to disperse once the advance began. The 38th Battalion was the third in position, suffering a number of casualties from German artillery which by this stage had registered the junction of 'K' Track and the sunken road as a lucrative target. Gas shells were also falling along the length of the track, but high winds meant these shells had little impact other than forcing the troops to wear gas masks with all the discomfort and disorientation that accompanied this. The 39th Battalion was the last 10th Brigade battalion to move into place, taking five hours to complete a journey that in better times an unimpeded tourist would have completed in one. The 39th Battalion occupied a position behind the 38th Battalion, at a sunken road near Hamburg Farm.

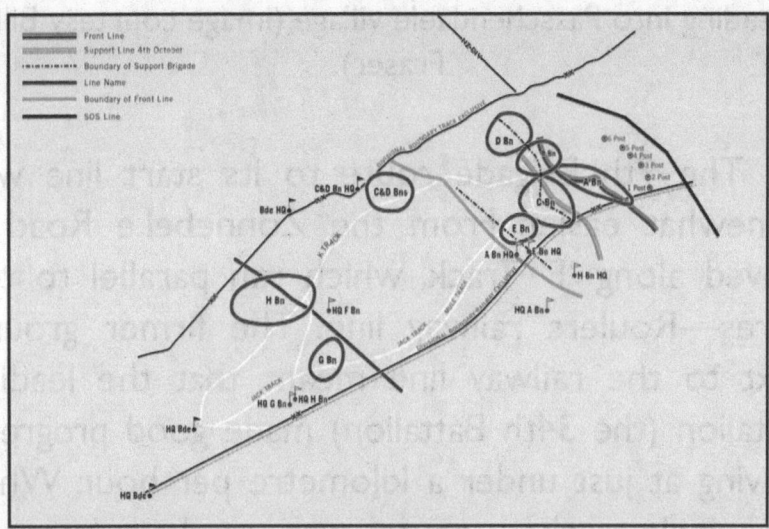

Map 12. Original map showing 'K' Track and Jack Track leading to the new front line on 16 October 1917. The 10th Brigade followed the duckboarded 'K' Track to its start line on 12 October 1917. It is probable that the Mule Track would have been close to, or on the actual 'F' Track which was the route followed by the 9th Brigade to its start line on 12 October 1917.

Remains of the Ypres—Roulers railway line in 2018 at the point just before it crosses the main road (Passendalestraat)

leading into Passchendaele village (image courtesy Bill Fraser).

The 9th Brigade route to its start line was somewhat easier. From the Zonnebeke Road it moved along 'F' Track, which ran parallel to the Ypres—Roulers railway line. The firmer ground next to the railway line meant that the leading battalion (the 34th Battalion) made good progress, moving at just under a kilometre per hour. While the single-tracked route was marked by tape strung on stakes a metre high, as the battalion reached Zonnebeke railway station it was subjected to heavy German artillery fire which inflicted casualties and destroyed a number of the guide posts and tape causing some delay. Despite these difficulties, the 34th Battalion managed to reach its start line by 2.45am. The rate of progress for the following battalions (35th, 36th, and 33rd) slowed, with the passage of troops and rain degrading the track until the mud was knee deep. While the 35th Battalion reached its start line without incident, the 36th experienced heavier shelling, including gas, during its approach march. The gas shells required the men to sporadically don their gas masks, increasing the difficulty of walking along the route in the dark. The artillery also inflicted casualties, with the 36th Battalion losing one officer and

100 men, the leading company of the battalion not reaching its start line until 4.48am. Moreover, elements of the Reserve Company of the 36th Battalion were delayed due to the ill-discipline of some 12th Brigade troops (those on the right flank of the 9th Brigade) who ignored the divisional boundaries and walked along the track reserved for the 9th Brigade. As a consequence, the Reserve Company did not reach its position behind the rest of the 36th Battalion until after zero hour, with the remainder of the battalion in place just before the barrage opened at 5.21am.

Despite these difficulties, by 4.00am the bulk of both brigades lay in position. In a reminder of the slow passage of information on the 1917 battlefield, and how difficult it was for higher headquarters to control a battle once it had commenced, Monash was unable to pass this information to Headquarters II ANZAC Corps until 6.54am—well after the opening of the attacking barrage at 5.25am. In the dark hours between 4.00am and the commencement of the barrage, the soldiers of the battalions lay on their start lines waiting for the attack to commence. Lieutenant McNicol of the 37th Battalion described the scene:

> About 3a.m. the rain began to fall steadily and in the sodden shell-holes the

waiting men became wet and chilled to the bone. To make matters worse, heavy shelling began to fall just in rear of our position. Huddled together in small groups, silent, thoughtful, and miserable, men needed all their powers of endurance that night.

This sentiment was shared throughout the two brigades. A member of the 39th Battalion, which was sheltering in the sunken road, recorded:

> Zero hour was still two hours ahead. Continuous heavy rain fell the whole time and the Germans kept up a bombardment along the sunken road. Little shrapnel was used, and the ground was so soft that shells buried themselves before exploding. But for this circumstance, the waiting troops would have been decimated before the battle began. As it was, heavy casualties resulted. The men longed for zero hour, preferring activity to a passive submission to a heavy bombardment.

THE BARRAGE COMMENCES

It was thus with some relief that the waiting troops watched the commencement of the Allied barrage at 5.25am. This would appear to have been some 35 minutes earlier than the

Broodseinde battle, but in reality it was 25 minutes later, as daylight saving had ceased with the onset of winter. Bean described the commencement of the barrage:

> ...when the British barrage descended, a whitish streak on the eastern horizon was lighting the low, dun-coloured, fleeting scud overhead and the dull, green and brown moorland below. Despite its imposing sound, the barrage, as on October 9th, afforded no screen and only light protection; all day it was possible to see clearly through it, and the attacking troops had difficulty in judging whether the scattered shells that burst fitfully around them were their own or the enemy's.

Bean was not the only observer to note the inadequate nature of the opening Allied barrage. Compared to previous attacks, soldiers in the battalions described the barrage as so thin that '. it could not be distinguished as a barrage' or it was dismissed as '...no more than desultory fire'. These personal observations were echoed in the 9th Brigade post-operational report, in which the barrage was described as being so weak it was difficult to discern the Allied barrage from the German counter-barrage. Adverse observations on the barrage were repeated in Monash's initial report of the battle to

Headquarters II ANZAC Corps on 14 October in which, based on interviews with survivors, Monash wrote '...the barrage was very thin and seemed to have no effect on silencing the enemy's machine gun defence.' These sentiments were repeated on 1 November when, in his official post-operational report, Monash described the barrage as totally inadequate. There can be little doubt that the barrage did not have the intensity of those fired in earlier battles. The cost of this inadequacy would be borne by the infantry.

Soldiers in the leading battalions braced themselves to push forward in the knowledge that the barrage was insufficient and that the German defences would not be fully suppressed. With no obvious barrage line to follow, their most basic control measure for determining their rate and direction of advance was also no longer effective. The increased risks resulting from the thin barrage would undoubtedly have played on their minds as they steeled themselves to go 'over the top'. Preparing to face fear at the start of an attack was an individual experience and, while mateship and being part of a battalion family helped, each man had to come to terms with his own fear. Padre George Cuttriss of the 43rd Battalion wrote of the human response to going 'over the top':

A peculiar sensation creeps annoyingly slowly along the spinal column, subtly affecting every member of the body. There's a gripping of the heart and a numbing of the brain, and the tongue persistently cleaves to the roof of the mouth, which seems as dry as powdered chalk. A choking sensation accompanies every effort to cough ... The seconds tick slowly by, the minutes are leaden-footed in their passing, and seem like eternities. The eyes are almost blinded through the strain of peering into darkness, the imagination runs riot, grotesque shapes are conjured into view, only to be dissipated by a solitary flare or a series of gun flashes.

At 5.25am on 12 October 1917 the soldiers of the 10th and 9th infantry brigades of the 3rd Australian Division, tired and cold from an arduous approach march and depleted in numbers by German artillery fire, rose from their start lines, shook out into attack formations and commenced their advance on Passchendaele.

THE 10TH BRIGADE: 5.25AM UNTIL NOON

The 37th Battalion, with a collective strength of 427, was the first 'over the top' and almost immediately drew German machine-gun fire from positions in Augustus Wood to the front and Waterfields to the left flank. German fire was heavy, and took advantage of the fact that the leading companies in the battalion began to bunch up as they moved towards Augustus Wood. The reason for this bunching was not obvious, but could have been the result of the channelling effect of a low line of barbed wire that ran diagonally across the axis of advance. Regardless of the reason, the German machine-gunners capitalised on this bunching with an eyewitness describing the men of the battalion as '...swept down in dozens'.

Despite the carnage wreaked by the German machine-guns, it seems that very little close combat took place. The battalion war diary states that those German soldiers the Australians encountered at the point of a bayonet surrendered readily, preferring captivity to death. In this regard, the message Monash sent to II ANZAC Corps Headquarters differed from the battalion account. At 8.48am he wrote: 'Left Brigade report large numbers of enemy have been killed with the bayonet during advance to the red line.'

The battalion war diary provided a more accurate report, if for no other reason than it would have been difficult for Monash to know what was actually happening in the close-quarter battle at the time he wrote his report. The implications of German infantry surrendering without a fight were significant, since this would have been evidence to support Haig's viewpoint that the German Army at Passchendaele was close to collapse. Unfortunately the veracity of this belief, at least for the 10th Brigade, was rarely tested. The German infantry did the majority of their killing from a distance, their superior firepower preventing the Australians closing with them.

The terrain of the Waterfields battlefield in 2018 (image courtesy of Bill Frost).

Regardless of the actual nature of the fighting, the battalion was suffering increasing casualties. Of the battalion officers, one had been killed and 11 wounded, but the troops pushed on and, by 7.00am, they had secured the battalion's Red Line objective. The ground at the objective was considered unsuited to a defensive position, so the battalion dug in some 45 metres short of the Red Line where it continued to be subjected to machine-gun and sniper fire. Battalion Headquarters was located to the rear at Hamburg Farm, which by this stage had become a focal point for German heavy artillery. In spite of two direct hits on the farm, communications between the headquarters and the rest of the battalion remained largely uninterrupted.

With the 37th Battalion having secured the Red Line it was now the turn of the 40th Battalion to pass through the 37th and capture the Blue Line. At the very outset this battalion also came under heavy machine-gun fire making it necessary for the men to move forward in bounds, seeking cover as they moved from shell hole to shell hole. The battalion also took heavy fire from Augustus Wood and D Company was detached to assist the 37th Battalion to mop up the German positions in the wood, capturing a number of German prisoners who were then used to carry wounded Australians back to the rear. This requirement, combined with the need to move forward in bounds, saw the battalion assault formation gradually disintegrate.

MAJOR LYNDHURST FALKINER GIBLIN, DSO, MC

Born in Hobart in 1872, the son of a local barrister, Lyndhurst Giblin was educated at The Hutchins School, Hobart, and University College, London. He entered King's College, Cambridge, in 1893, graduating with a maths and science degree. He represented King's College and Cambridge at rowing and rugby and also played rugby for England. After graduation he went prospecting for gold in British Columbia. Finding little gold, he worked as a lumberman before joining a schooner sailing back to Australia in 1904. After a brief trip to Solomon Islands in 1905, he returned to Hobart to teach mathematics. In 1909 he ran unsuccessfully for the Tasmanian Parliament, before joining the Labor Party and winning a seat in the Tasmanian House of Assembly between 1913 and 1915. In 1909 he had been commissioned as a lieutenant in the Intelligence Corps, was promoted to captain and transferred to the 40th Battalion, AIF, in 1916. He was wounded at both Armentieres and Messines and won the Military Cross in August 1917. Promoted to major he won the Distinguished Service Order in June 1918, but was wounded again in August at Bapaume, ending his war service. Returning to Australia he was the Government Statistician of Tasmania from 1919 to 1928 and Acting Commonwealth Statistician from 1931 to 1932. He was also a member of the Commonwealth Grants Commission between 1922 and 1936, a Director of the Commonwealth Bank between 1935 and 1942 and Chairman of the Commonwealth Financial and Economic Committee from 1939 to 1946. He died in Hobart in 1951.

A group portrait of the officers of the 40th Battalion at Neuve Église, Belgium, on 26 January 1918. Major Lyndhurst Giblin is seated in the front row, third from the right (AWM E01610).

Despite these difficulties the battalion continued to move forward until it took machine-gun and sniper fire from the entrenchments and pillboxes on the Bellevue spur, which inflicted heavy casualties. In a somewhat optimistic gesture, a platoon from D Company was detached to try to deal with this flanking fire from the spur which, under the II ANZAC Corps plan, was the responsibility of the New Zealand Division to neutralise. The rest of the battalion arrived on the Red Line at around 7.45am in groups of two and three, with all companies intermingled. Of the 450 soldiers who left the battalion start line, approximately 150 arrived on the Red Line, where they waited behind the Red Line protective barrage.

The advance to the Blue Line was due to commence at 8.25am, but a quick assessment of the battalion's position by Major Lyndhurst Giblin, a surviving company commander, soon revealed the impossibility of achieving this. Giblin was an experienced officer, having won a Military Cross at Messines and a Distinguished Service Order at Broodseinde, and was well equipped to assess the situation. With the battalion's left flank fully exposed and vulnerable to German fire from the Bellevue spur, and the disposition of the 9th Brigade troops on his right flank unclear, Giblin had no choice but to organise the remaining troops into a defensive position. Runners were sent back to Battalion Headquarters at Berlin Wood reporting this course of action and also advising that any further advance was impossible without the New Zealand Division clearing the Bellevue spur.

A view of the swamp-like conditions associated with the creeks of the Ypres salient, 12 October 1917. Since the ruins of the Zonnebeke church can be seen in the background, this photograph is possibly to the east of Zonnebeke, near the Zonnebeke-Steenbeek creek system and would have been indicative of the ground around Ravebeek Creek (AWM E01200).

With the survivors of both the 37th and 40th battalions dug in around the Red Line, the chances of the 38th Battalion advancing beyond this line were slim. Like the two previous battalions, the 38th had started to take heavy casualties from the Bellevue spur the moment it left its start line. Like the 40th Battalion, the 38th also sent a platoon across Ravebeek Creek in an attempt to deal with the enfilade fire. The creek proved to be a difficult but not impassable obstacle and the platoon managed to clear three German pillboxes, but was soon pinned down by fire. The men were forced to remain under cover until nightfall when they returned to join the main body of the battalion. The remainder of the battalion continued their advance to the Red Line where they began to dig defensive positions along with the survivors of the 37th and 40th battalions.

The 10th Brigade messages sent to Divisional Headquarters indicated that the battalion had advanced beyond the Red Line, but did not specify how far. At 9.20am Monash sent a message to II ANZAC Corps Headquarters reporting that the battalion had crossed the Red Line between 8.00 and 10.00am and that all was going well. This assessment is at odds with the battalion diary and the confusion may have arisen from the fact that Major Giblin had moved the remnants of the two earlier battalions some 45 metres to the rear of the Red Line. He had done this because part of the original Red Line featured a prominent tree which the Germans were using as an artillery marker.

The Church of St Audomarus in Passchendaele after its complete rebuilding in the post-war period (image courtesy of Bill Frost).

In one of those strange incidents of war, a small party of 20 men, largely from the 38th Battalion, moved unnoticed and untouched by German fire up Ravebeek Creek gully. A 10th Brigade report after the battle stated that this party was led by Major Giblin but, given that he was busy organising the brigade defence, this was unlikely. Whoever was leading this group confronted a German pillbox near the apex of the gully at Crest Farm, but all the German soldiers manning the position quickly surrendered without a fight. Glancing over to the Bellevue spur, the Australians could see large numbers of Germans retreating during the early stages of the New Zealand Division's attack. Encouraged by what they must have believed to be a German rout, the party proceeded until they reached what seemed to be a deserted church at the centre of Passchendaele. Without support and in an isolated position, they soon withdrew to join the left flank of the 9th Brigade. As they did, they noted that, after their initial fright, the Germans were reoccupying their positions on the Bellevue spur and at Crest Farm.

Unaware of this opportunity, 10th Brigade Headquarters could do little to exploit it. The 39th Battalion was the Brigade Reserve and had already provided an additional company to the 40th Battalion and had another company allocated as a brigade carrying party. Reduced to two fully effective infantry companies, the battalion's ability as the Brigade Reserve to reverse the fortunes of the brigade was slim to non-existent. In the confusion associated with the failure of the first three battalion attacks, groups of 39th Battalion men had not moved forward and remained bunched up behind captured German pillboxes. The battalion's Commanding Officer, Lieutenant Colonel Robert Henderson, a veteran of Messines and Broodseinde, took control of the situation and organised two lieutenants (both of whom shortly became casualties) to take charge of the men and move them forward. Once Lieutenant

Colonel Henderson became aware of the debacle with the three forward battalions, he reported the situation to Brigadier General McNicoll, seeking clarification on the employment of the Brigade Reserve. Following Monash's orders, McNicoll sent the battalion to assist in securing the Red Line, which was all it could reasonably be expected to achieve.

THE NEW ZEALAND DIVISION AND THE BELLEVUE SPUR

The failure of the 10th Brigade to advance beyond the Red Line was largely due to the enfilade fire coming from the Bellevue spur. This fire decimated the attacking battalions and, while the 40th and 38th battalions each sent a platoon across Ravebeek Creek to deal with the enfilade fire, the strength of the German positions meant that they had little prospect of success. Under the II ANZAC Corps plan, clearance of the Bellevue spur was the responsibility of the New Zealand Division. The planners realised, quite rightly as events would show, that any attack on Passchendaele that involved an approach between the Bellevue spur and Passchendaele Ridge would only succeed if both geographic features were secured. In this regard the fortunes of the 10th

Brigade and the New Zealand Division were inextricably linked.

At the start of the attack, the New Zealand Division had formed a front along the line Marsh Bottom—Peter Pan—Yetta House with Ravebeek Creek marking the divisional boundary between the New Zealand Division and the 3rd Australian Division. As stated, the primary objective of the New Zealand Division was the capture of the Bellevue—Meetcheele—Goudberg spur. The New Zealand plan had two brigades leading the attack, each with a frontage of approximately 700 metres, with the 2nd New Zealand Brigade sharing a boundary with the 10th Brigade. With such a narrow frontage, the attack by the 2nd New Zealand Brigade would be conducted by a series of battalions in echelon with each securing an individual objective—the same tactic being used by the Australian brigades.

The New Zealand Division had one hundred and forty-four 18-pounders and forty-eight 4.5-inch howitzers in direct support; but, like the Australians, the effectiveness of its artillery was limited by the muddy conditions, which had adversely affected munitions supply. More significantly, the mud restricted the ability to move the artillery forward to fire on the German positions further to the rear and, by the afternoon of 11 October, the only guns sited well forward comprised a mix of eight 18-pounders and 4.5-inch howitzers. The artillery had insufficient time or munitions to deal with the Germans around the Bellevue spur, which was a formidable position since it was at the junction of the Flanders Line I and Flanders Line II. Reconnaissance patrols on the night of 10 October soon ascertained that the German barbed-wire obstacles on the Bellevue spur were largely intact. Heavy artillery was allocated to pound the wire on the morning of 11 October, but this proved insufficient to cause significant breaches in the German obstacles.

When the Allied barrage commenced firing for the New Zealanders at 5.25am it would prove just as ineffective as that supporting the Australians. As the barrage moved up the Bellevue spur towards the German pillboxes it diminished in intensity, doing little to suppress the German machine-guns. Despite the desultory artillery fire, the initial New Zealand advance proceeded satisfactorily, with parties of German troops seen fleeing without their arms over the skyline of the spur. Once the New Zealanders reached the largely unbroken German barbed wire on the western slopes of the spur the advance slowed, encouraging the previously panicked German soldiers to return and man their weapons. Trapped in German barbed-wire obstacles some 22 to 45 metres in depth and taking heavy casualties, the New Zealand troops could do little but dig themselves defensive positions and, by 9.00am, the majority of forward movement had ceased. The failure to clear the Bellevue spur meant that the left flank of the 10th Brigade was completely exposed to German fire, effectively ending any chance of the brigade proceeding beyond its Red Line.

THE 9TH BRIGADE: 5.25AM UNTIL NOON

The 34th Battalion led the 9th Brigade attack. Like their colleagues in the 37th Battalion, the men of the 34th soon discovered that the heavy ground conditions slowed their advance. Conditions were worse on the left flank of the 34th Battalion since it was closer to Ravebeek Creek. Even on the right flank, despite the presence of firmer ground near the railway line, men who sought cover in shell holes required assistance to extricate themselves from the bogs at the bottom of the holes. The first German resistance they encountered was a pair of pillboxes east of Augustus Wood and north-east of Heine House, consisting of four machine-guns and a garrison of 35 German soldiers. Some 140 metres behind these pillboxes was a German trench line containing 20 to 30 supporting troops. These defensive positions held up the centre of the battalion advance until a bombing party led by Captain Clarence Jeffries, the Officer Commanding B Company, succeeded in rushing and capturing the German pillboxes, with the Germans in the reserve trench captured shortly afterwards.

MAJOR GENERAL SIR ANDREW HAMILTON RUSSELL, KCB, KCMG

Born in Napier, New Zealand, in 1868, Andrew Russell was the son of an English officer who came to New Zealand with the 58th Regiment. He was educated in England and won entry to the Royal Military College, Sandhurst, in 1886. After graduation he served in the 1st Battalion, the Border Regiment, in India and Burma from 1887 to 1892. Resigning his commission, he returned to New Zealand to take up farming, but in 1900 formed and commanded the Hawke's Bay Mounted Rifles Volunteers. He held a number of militia positions and, with the formation of the 1st New Zealand Expeditionary Force in 1914, was appointed to command of the New Zealand Mounted Rifles Brigade during the Gallipoli campaign. In November 1915 Russell was promoted and took over command of the New Zealand and Australian Division from Alexander Godley. He went on to command the New Zealand Division from May 1916 until the end of the war. Russell blamed himself for the heavy losses suffered by his division at Passchendaele and worked hard to restore his men's morale following the battle. He played a significant role in defeating the German 1918 Spring Offensive and Haig offered him a corps command in June 1918. However the war ended before this offer could be realised. Following the Armistice, Russell returned to farming but suffered from poor health. He became President of the New Zealand Returned Soldiers' Association from 1921 to 1924 and again from 1926 to 1935. While his bid to enter parliament in 1922 was unsuccessful, he remained prominent in a number of conservative causes. With the onset of the Second World War he was appointed Inspector-General of the Forces, resigning from this position in July 1941, although he remained on the War Council until 1942. Russell died in 1960 at the age of 92.

Major General Andrew Russell sitting in a wicker chair at the New Zealand Divisional Headquarters in the village of Bus-Les Artois, the Somme, 21 May 1918 (National Library of New Zealand, Ref: 1/1-002064-G).

Near Broodseinde, men and horse struggle to move an 18 pounder and limber through the mud during preparations for the 12 October attack (AWM E01208).

CAPTAIN CLARENCE SMITH JEFFERIES VC

Born in Newcastle in 1894, Clarence Jefferies was the only child of Joshua Jefferies, a colliery manager, and his wife Barbara. He attended Dudley Primary School and Newcastle High School before being apprenticed to his father as a mining engineer. He joined the 14th (Hunter River) Infantry Regiment at the age of 14 as a private and was commissioned in

August 1914. He spent the early years of the war as a lieutenant training AIF recruits before being appointed as a second lieutenant in the 34th Battalion, AIF, on 1 February 1916. After five months' training in Britain, Jefferies and his battalion moved to the Western Front. His first major action was at the Battle of Messines in June 1917 where, while leading a reconnaissance patrol, Jefferies was shot in the thigh. Evacuated to London, he recovered, was promoted to captain and rejoined his battalion in September 1917 as a company commander. During the 9th Brigade attack on 12 October 1917 Jefferies performed a series of actions that saw him awarded a posthumous Victoria Cross. His medal citation was posted in the London *Gazette* on 18 December 1917 and reads in part:

> For most conspicuous bravery in attack, when his company was held up by enemy machine gun fire from concrete emplacements. Organising a party, he rushed one emplacement, capturing four machine guns and thirty-five prisoners. He then led his company forward under extremely heavy enemy artillery barrage and enfilade machine gun fire to the objective. Later, he again organised a successful attack on a machine gun emplacement,

capturing two machine guns and thirty more prisoners. This gallant officer was killed during the attack, but it was entirely due to his bravery and initiative that the centre of the attack was not held up for a lengthy period. His example had a most inspiring influence.

Due to the heavy nature of the fighting, Jefferies' body was not immediately identified or recovered from the battlefield. In 1920 his father set out for Belgium to find his son's grave, but to no avail. It was not until January 1921 that Joshua Jefferies learnt that his son's body had been exhumed from another grave, correctly identified and reburied in the Tyne Cot Commonwealth War Graves Cemetery. Joshua Jefferies made another trip to Belgium in 1924 and was finally able to visit his son's grave.

Studio portrait of Lieutenant Clarence Jeffries taken in Newcastle, New South Wales, in 1916 prior to his embarkation for Britain (AWM P09373.001).

Having reached the Red Line, the forward elements of the battalion began to dig in, but continued to take fire from a German position on the right flank, 200 yards from the railway embankment. While the troublesome position lay outside his area of operational responsibility, such technicalities did not constrain Jefferies. Again he organised an ad hoc assault party, this time consisting of two non-commissioned officers (NCOs) and 10 men, and set off to silence the German position. While the attack was a success and resulted in the capture of two machine-guns and 30 prisoners, Jefferies was killed in the assault. He was awarded the Victoria Cross for his bravery in these two actions.

The German machine-guns that killed Jefferies were within the divisional boundary of the 4th Australian Division, which was tasked with securing the right flank of the 9th Brigade. The 12th Brigade was the unit that had been given this responsibility and advanced with two battalions (47th Battalion leading and 48th Battalion in the rear), using the Ypres—Roulers railway line as their left boundary. During the process of overcoming German resistance the two battalions intermingled, but successfully secured the Red Line. Any advance beyond this line was considered impossible due to heavy German fire coming from Tiber Copse. Later that day confusion would arise between the two brigades as to the extent of the 9th Brigade advance, the 12th Brigade believing that the 9th never left the Red Line when in fact the 9th had secured part of the Blue Line.

In the 9th Brigade the leadership of the 34th Battalion had largely devolved to the NCOs, as all but three commissioned officers had been killed or wounded. One of the survivors, the Officer Commanding D Company, Captain J.W. Richardson, had reorganised the remnants of the battalion ready to take it forward to assist the 35th Battalion in the capture of the Blue Line. However he was also killed during the subsequent advance.

While the troops of the 34th Battalion dug in on the Red Line, the 35th Battalion had been following closely behind, helping to mop up German troops sheltering in their dugouts, many of which remained undamaged due to the ineffective nature of the Allied barrage. By the time the 35th Battalion reached the Red Line and joined the 34th, both battalions had suffered heavy casualties and had become intermingled, leading to a loss of unit cohesion.

The 36th Battalion was the third battalion in echelon and the one tasked with capturing the Green Line. It soon caught up with the 34th and 35th battalions and, after waiting for the

Allied barrage, all three battalions commenced their advance towards the Blue Line. They had not moved far before they encountered heavy machine-gun fire to their immediate front from Crest Farm and Passchendaele and to their left from the Bellevue spur. The left-hand company of the 36th Battalion was decimated and the Commanding Officer, Gallipoli veteran Lieutenant Colonel John Milne, directed another company to fill the gap. While the Blue Line was secured, the failure of the 10th Brigade to advance further than the Red Line had placed the battalion in a precarious position, its left flank totally exposed. Undeterred by these setbacks, Milne gathered all available men from the Red Line and combined these with his Reserve Company in a desperate attempt to capture the Green Line. As they moved forward, German fire soon produced heavy casualties and it became clear that the attempt would have to be abandoned.

The 33rd Battalion was the 9th Brigade reserve and began its battle in a state of confusion. D Company and two platoons of B Company went missing, having inadvertently advanced with the barrage instead of waiting in reserve with the rest of the battalion. By 10.22am the battalion had received orders to advance and occupy a defensive position in the vicinity of the Red Line. As it remained in reserve and waited for further orders, the battalion took so many casualties from German artillery fire that it was forced to amalgamate B and D companies.

THE SITUATION AT NOON

By late morning confusion over the disposition of the two brigades had begun to dissipate and the situation was now clearer. On the left flank the 10th Brigade had taken heavy losses, particularly from the German positions on the Bellevue spur, but had managed to secure the Red Line with the survivors digging in some 140 metres to the rear of the actual line. The failure of the New Zealand Division to clear the Bellevue spur continued to expose the left flank of the brigade and, even had there been sufficient troops available to consider a further advance, the unsecured flank would have made such an attack problematic. On the right flank the 9th Brigade enjoyed greater success. It had secured the Red Line and part of the Blue Line, but its right flank was only partially protected by the 4th Australian Division, which had halted at the Red Line. It was not until late afternoon (around 5.00pm) that the 12th Brigade became aware that the 9th Brigade had reached the Blue Line. The failure of the 10th and 12th brigades to advance beyond the Red Line meant that both flanks of the 9th Brigade were exposed. The 9th Brigade attack had also culminated and, without significant reinforcements, was unlikely to advance beyond the Blue Line. The 11th Brigade remained to the rear of both attacking brigades, tasked with securing the front line and providing a firm base for the attack.

The mud was having an obvious impact on the infantry's ability to keep pace with the Allied barrage but, perversely, this was not a critical failure since the barrage was doing little to suppress the German defences. The mud also constrained the forward movement of the heavier infantry support weapons such as the Stokes mortars and the Vickers machine-guns. Many of these weapons had not moved far beyond their respective start lines, denying the advancing battalions any weapons capable of suppressing the long-range German machinegun or sniper fire. The swampy ground of the Ravebeek Creek was an effective obstacle and the closer the troops pushed to the creek the slower their movement. But events had also shown that the creek could be crossed, even while under fire. Monash noted that the '...Swamp in D.11.C [Ravebeek Creek] proved a serious obstacle but apparently has been overcome.

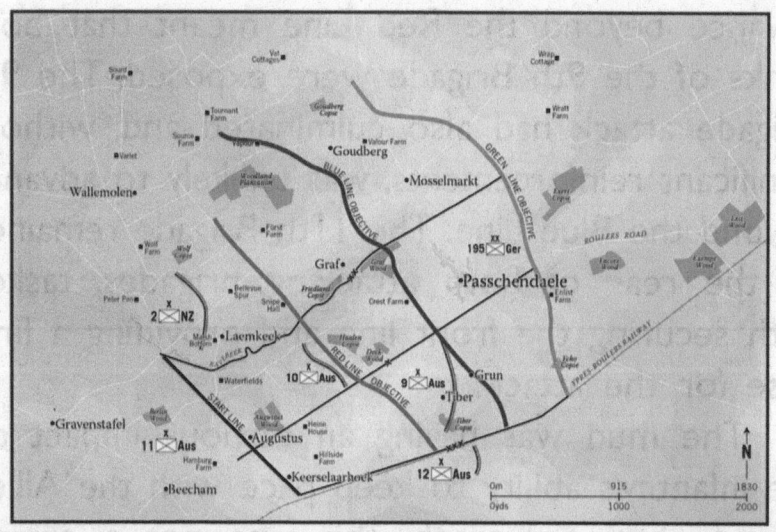

Map 13. Allied dispositions at noon on 12 October 1917. The New Zealand Division's 2nd Brigade had been ensnared by the German wire in front of the Bellevue spur and had halted under heavy fire. The 10th Brigade had sustained heavy losses and was digging in some 140 metres short of the Red Line. Elements of the 9th Brigade had reached the Blue Line, but were under extreme pressure from German artillery batteries to their front. Both the left and right flanks of the 9th Brigade were exposed. The 4th Australian Division's 12th Brigade had reached the Red Line but had culminated. Both the 10th and 9th brigades were taking heavy and sustained enfilade fire from German defensive positions on the Bellevue spur.

If there was one feature that was determining the course of the battle it was the Bellevue spur. Indeed mud, artillery and the Bellevue spur were now intertwined in an unholy alliance. The mud had prevented the implementation of an effective artillery fire plan, which meant that the barbed wire in front of the Bellevue spur remained uncut, preventing the New Zealand Division advancing on the feature. With the New Zealand Division trapped in the barbed wire at the foot of the spur, German machine-guns were now firing at right angles directly into the left flank of the 3rd Australian Division. This fire continued to cause casualties and make any forward movement difficult if not impossible. Unless the German positions on the Bellevue spur could be captured or suppressed by artillery fire, both of which were unlikely, the chances of Monash's division capturing Passchendaele were diminishing by the minute.

For Monash, this realisation would come slowly. His flow of information from the forward battalions, normally provided by battalion runners, was curtailed by the heavy German shelling which prevented runners from getting back to battalion and then brigade headquarters with any frequency. Battlefield reports from the forward units were being provided by carrier pigeons and aerial observation, the latter not helped by the shooting down of one of the dedicated liaison aircraft from 21 Squadron. Nevertheless, Monash produced a steady stream of handwritten notes reporting on the battle to Headquarters II ANZAC Corps. The early notes were optimistic:

7.57am Advance was proceeding steadily at six o'clock a.m. Over 100 prisoners already on way in add. Many enemy Machine Guns opened at zero.—and believe all going well.

8.28am Fairly reliably reported that we are digging in on red line along my whole front.

9.20am Left Brigade reports battalion for blue objective passed over red line at 8-10am and all of them going well.

9.32am Both Brigades report advance from red to blue line has been successfully launched.

10.30am Unconfirmed report that my left Brigade is on blue line.

By 11.00am Monash's reporting had become more pessimistic. As more accurate reports arrived, the impact of the German fire from the Bellevue spur on his division gradually became clearer:

10.57am Observers with telescope report seeing our troops [10th Brigade] moving forward near Crest Farm at 10.20am. My advance suffering heavily from M.G. fire from spur...

11.21am In view of situation on my left flank I have ordered my left Brigade to employ its reserve Battalion [39th Battalion] to assist securing all ground won, and am holding one Battalion of my Divisional Reserve in readiness to support my left Brigade.

The issue for Monash was what to do about the deteriorating position on his left flank. Between 10.40am and 11.55am, in an attempt to regain control of the battle, he sent a series of notes to his brigade commanders concerning the condition and location of the battalions constituting their Brigade Reserve. He authorised the 10th Brigade to use its Reserve Battalion (39th Battalion) to secure that ground already captured and then to hold the Red Line. The 9th Brigade was permitted to retain its Reserve Battalion (33rd Battalion) for its own use, but it could not be committed without Monash's approval. This approval was given at 11.55am when it was released to support the 34th Battalion. The 11th Brigade was directed to nominate one battalion and hold it in readiness to become a reserve for the 10th Brigade. Like the 33rd Battalion, this unit was not to move without Monash's express approval.

By 11.00am Godley had ordered Major General Andrew Russell, GOC New Zealand Division, to suspend his attack and prepare for a new attack later that afternoon. Monash had earlier explored the possibility of pushing the

New Zealand Division's reserve through the 10th Brigade area to '...deal with the situation'. Whether Monash first approached Godley about requesting the New Zealand reserve is uncertain, but an hour earlier Monash had certainly been in touch with Russell to elicit New Zealand assistance for the 40th Battalion. It is unclear whether Monash intended the New Zealanders to launch a right-flank attack on the Bellevue spur across Ravebeek Creek or assist the 10th Brigade advance to the Green Line. What is clear is that the New Zealand Division was not in any state to assist Monash.

THE DECISION—ADVANCE, HOLD OR WITHDRAW?

By midday three options were available to Godley and II ANZAC Corps: regroup and continue the attack mid-afternoon; stabilise a new front line based on the Red Line and continue the attack at a later date; or call of the attack and withdraw to the start line. There were pre-existing Corps plans for a pause and then a renewed attack should both divisions reach the Blue Line, but none existed for the current situation. For Godley, the key to success was the capture of the Bellevue spur by the 2nd New Zealand Brigade. With the 10th Brigade holding the Red Line and the 9th Brigade on the Blue Line, a successful advance by the New Zealanders still held some promise of victory—an opportunity that Godley was determined to explore. After ordering the halt of the New Zealand attack at 11.00am, he directed Russell's men to prepare for a new attack at 3.00pm, supported by the Allied barrage that would be brought back to the Red Line. However Russell, who had received reports from the 2nd New Zealand Brigade Major, was less than enthusiastic. His battalion commanders were unanimous in their opinion that the proposed attack should be abandoned. Not only had they suffered some 3000 casualties, but the German barbed wire remained unbroken. Having dug in among the barbed-wire entanglements, the New Zealand troops were now too close to the wire for a successful bombardment to be safely fired. If an attack was to be conducted, the troops would have to withdraw in daylight, under German fire, to reorganise and reassemble prior to advancing back over ground they had just evacuated. Russell told Corps Headquarters that, unless a heavy bombardment could be brought down on the spur, his exhausted and depleted troops could not launch a further attack.

The situation in the 3rd Australian Division was little better. Monash's ability to renew the attack from within his division's resources was limited by the fact that he had no uncommitted troops in his two forward brigades. This left the 11th Brigade as his last available manoeuvre unit. While not directly involved in the assault, the brigade was tasked with securing the front line against a German counter-attack which could push through the depleted 9th and 10th brigades. The likelihood of such a bold German response increased as the day wore on. Since late morning, the 40th Battalion had been taking fire to its rear as German troops began working their way down the Bellevue spur in an attempt to infiltrate the captured ground between the 10th Brigade start line and the Red Line. Given this evolving threat, Monash had little option but to retain the majority of the 11th Brigade as his division's firm base.

If Monash still held any prospect for victory it was with the 9th Brigade, which he believed still had an opportunity to secure Crest Farm and then advance on Passchendaele. Shortly after 2.00pm he sent an order to the 11th Brigade ordering it to detach the 41st Battalion to support the 10th Brigade and the 43rd Battalion to support the 9th Brigade. The 43rd Battalion would be used with the 33rd in an attempt to capture Crest Farm, with the operation due to commence at 4.56pm. This attack was never launched. Based on Russell's advice on the state of the New Zealand Division, Godley had no choice but to cancel his proposed 3.00pm attack. Once this was decided, any further attack by Monash made no sense since his left and right flanks remained unsupported and his division was increasingly vulnerable to German counter-attack. As is often the case in battle, the reality on the ground was now dictating that the only available course of action was a withdrawal to the division's start line.

THE 10TH BRIGADE'S WITHDRAWAL

By early afternoon the 10th Brigade occupied defensive positions some 140 metres to the rear of the Red Line, where Major Giblin had moved the troops earlier in the morning. In the absence of any orders from Brigade Headquarters Giblin, now the most senior 10th Brigade officer in the front line, was again required to assess the situation. Several runners had been sent back seeking orders with all bar one falling to German sniper fire. In the absence of orders from Brigade Headquarters, Giblin held an impromptu conference with the surviving battalion officers to determine a course of action. They decided to withdraw to the brigade start line. Here contact could be re-established with the New Zealand Division and the German threat to the brigade's left flank nullified. The morally courageous nature of this decision is described in the 39th Battalion history:

> It was a serious decision, and they felt the responsibility keenly, especially as it was the Brigade's first reverse. If the senior officers further back had not agreed that the situation warranted such a retirement these ... officers might have been sent home to Australia in disgrace.

Notwithstanding their personal concerns, Giblin and the other officers had made their decision by 1.33pm. A basic plan was quickly developed and at 1.45pm orders were issued for the withdrawal. Conducting a withdrawal while in contact with the enemy is the most difficult of operations, but it is especially so when there are large numbers of wounded soldiers to be considered. The plan was to gradually thin out the defensive line, with small groups of four to five men moving in a staggered manner back to the vicinity of Augustus Wood. Carrying parties were organised to remove the wounded with the mud making this task particularly taxing. Even with eight men allocated per stretcher it was a struggle and every man who could be spared was pressed into this service.

The first batches of men sent to the rear were from the more secure right flank, and were led by two officers who helped organise the new defensive line. The withdrawal was spread out over an hour and attracted a good deal of German machine-gun and artillery fire which attempted to follow the groups of men as they were withdrawing. However the 39th Battalion reported that, once the Germans understood that some parties were attempting to carry wounded soldiers, the fire on these groups ceased. By 3.00pm the withdrawal was almost complete and the Germans, rather belatedly, heavily shelled the now almost vacant position, inflicting few casualties. By 3.30pm the brigade survivors had moved to a new defensive position in the sunken road—the position that had formed the assembly point of their original start line. To prevent infiltration and secure the left flank, patrols were sent to establish contact with the 2nd New Zealand Brigade. Recovery parties were also despatched to collect the dead and wounded, finally providing some relief to the 10th Brigade wounded and those men from the 66th British Division who had fallen in the Poelcappelle attack three days earlier.

THE 9TH BRIGADE'S WITHDRAWAL

Unlike the 10th Brigade, the 9th Brigade was spread out from the Blue Line with some semblance of a formation. The 36th Battalion was on the left, the 35th Battalion in the centre, the 34th Battalion on the right, with the designated Reserve Battalion (33rd Battalion) to the rear on the Red Line. The forward battalions had no contact with the 10th Brigade, but were in touch with a small party from the 12th Brigade on its right, even if the bulk of this brigade was still on the Red Line. The battalions had limited contact with 9th Brigade Headquarters, and with all carrier pigeons despatched or killed, runners were the only means of communication. Lieutenant Colonel John Milne, Commanding Officer of the 36th Battalion, was now in charge of the Blue Line battalions. He was not positioned on the Blue Line, but located at Hillside Farm, which was some 1200 metres to the rear of the Blue Line.

By 1.40pm Milne had managed to consolidate a defence across the entire frontage of the Blue Line, albeit on the forward edge of a slope. This exposed location provided German observers an uninterrupted view of the 9th Brigade position and saw machine-gun fire concentrated on the brigade from both flanks, along with fire from German artillery batteries located at Passchendaele and Enlist Farm—a range of just over 450 metres. Requests for reinforcements had seen all available men from the Red Line sent forward to reinforce the Blue Line but, given the intensity of the German fire, this was soon discontinued as it simply resulted in further casualties. The Brigade Reserve (the 33rd Battalion) remained on the Red Line for the time being, providing a firm base against a German counter-attack.

At 1.30pm Milne had received orders for the brigade to hold the Blue Line at all costs and link up with the 10th Brigade back on the Red Line. Two companies of the 33rd Battalion were also placed under Milne's direct command to be used in a counter-attack role. Despite these reinforcements, the brigade was in an invidious position. Exposed and under direct fire from German artillery, the likely outcome of continuing to hold its current position would be the gradual destruction of the brigade. Conferring under fire, Major Carr and Captain Dixon of the 35th Battalion and Captain Gadd of the 36th Battalion decided that Dixon and Gadd should return to Enlist Farm and inform Milne of the situation on the Blue Line. Milne listened to

Dixon and Gadd and told them that he would attempt to relieve the brigade after dark, but until then the troops would have to hold their ground.

At this stage the logic of defeat began to take its own course. Returning to the Blue Line at 3.15pm, Gadd agreed with Dixon that, while not withdrawing would ensure the brigade's destruction, Milne's order gave them no option but to hold on. Carr agreed to suspend any decision until they could again communicate with Milne and explain the brigade's dire circumstances, Dixon having gone to 35th Battalion Headquarters and not returned. At 3.45pm Carr and Gadd, unable to communicate with Milne, decided they could wait no longer and sent out a warning order for an impending withdrawal.

While the intensity of German fire was the immediate reason for Carr's warning order for a withdrawal, the uncertainty of the situation on the left flank must also have played its part. At 2.35pm the 35th Battalion reported that an unnamed officer of the 10th Brigade had indicated that his brigade was withdrawing. Since Giblin had issued the order for the 10th Brigade withdrawal at 1.45pm, this report was undoubtedly accurate, but it was not recognised as such. Unsure of its veracity, at 3.35pm 9th

Brigade Headquarters contacted its counterparts in the 10th Brigade, only to be promptly told that no withdrawal was taking place, despite the 10th Brigade withdrawal having been largely completed by 3.00pm.

Details on the actual conduct of the withdrawal are sketchy. In his post-action report on the battle, Milne simply states that: '...at dusk, Major Carr decided that it was impossible to hold on and a new line was formed from AUGUSTUS WOOD to intersection PASSCHENDAELE ROAD...' The unit diaries of the withdrawing battalions also provide little information in their reports, although a post-action report states that Carr was wounded in the shoulder during the withdrawal. At 3.00pm, some 45 minutes before Carr gave the warning order to withdraw, the Brigade Reserve Battalion (33rd Battalion) began to move back to a line near Augustus Wood, having received word (presumably sent by Carr since nobody else had made this decision) that the forward battalions were to withdraw.

CAPTAIN (TEMPORARY MAJOR) HENRY VINCE CARR

Henry Carr was born in Parramatta, New South Wales, in 1883, and was one of 14 children. Prior to the war he was a Commonwealth civil servant and had held a commission in the militia since 1908. Carr enlisted in the AIF in March 1916 at the age of 32 and was allocated to the 35th Battalion. Arriving in England in July 1916 he spent some months with the 9th and 10th training battalions before proceeding to France and joining the 35th Battalion in May 1917. He was wounded in the left shoulder at Passchendaele and evacuated to England. After a little over a month in hospital, he returned to France and rejoined his unit in December 1917. At First Villers-Bretonneux on 4 April 1918, Carr found himself in a similar situation to that of Passchendaele, being held responsible for failing to hold the line when circumstances were beyond his control. As at Passchendaele, Carr was cleared by an inquiry. In both battles he had acted bravely and conscientiously and this was recognised by his attendance at the Senior Officers' Course in France in June 1918. Carr was again wounded in action on 8 August 1918 during a 9th Brigade attack to take Accroche Wood and was evacuated to England. He did not return to his unit until after the Armistice, rejoining his men in December. He returned to Australia in October 1919, but before embarking completed some secretarial work with the Scottish Farmers' Workers Union. He was discharged from the AIF in March 1920 with the rank of honorary major. Little is known of Carr's post-war life other than that he divorced his wife in 1948 and subsequently remarried. He died in 1975 at a war veterans' nursing home aged 92.

Studio portrait taken in 1916 showing Captain Henry Carr (left) and Lieutenant Colonel Marcus Logan, Commanding Officer of the 35th Battalion from February to July 1916 (AWM 2016.183.4).

Wounded Australian soldiers, probably from the 9th Brigade, resting alongside dead German soldiers at the railway cutting on the Ypres-Roulers railway line, 12 October 1917 (AWM E04644).

Confusion over the conduct of a withdrawal is not a new phenomenon, particularly when a unit is under the intense pressure experienced by the 9th Brigade. However these circumstances did not prevent Carr's conduct of the withdrawal attracting condemnation. In his report to 3rd Australian Division Headquarters following the battle, the Brigade Major of the 9th Brigade was critical of Carr's actions, both for his decision to withdraw and the fact that the withdrawal extended as far as the brigade's start line rather than the Red Line. While the report conceded that holding the Blue Line would have been difficult, Carr received little dispensation for the fact that the 10th Brigade was already on its own start line, making any decision to hold on the Blue Line redundant.

Indirectly however, the report did provide Carr with a degree of justification since it admitted that the flow of battlefield information between battalion, brigade and division during the battle was less than optimal: '...better results would be obtained if Brigade Commanders could be in personal touch with their Battalion Commanders and thus promptly able to organise assistance where required.'

This concession was of little comfort to Carr who, having been given orders to hold an unsustainable position, with promises of a possible relief at nightfall, exercised his judgement in deciding to withdraw the brigade to the only viable defensive position—that of the brigade's original start line. Carr's wounding and subsequent evacuation to England appeared to be all that saved him from any disciplinary charges since the second-last paragraph of the report states: 'It would appear Major Carr erred in his orders for withdrawal, but as that officer is absent wounded it would be unfair to make any charge against him.'

A court of inquiry, chaired by Lieutenant Colonel Morshead, was constituted on 21 December 1917 to investigate the withdrawal of the 9th Brigade. While Carr's actions were not the stated subject of the inquiry, there was little doubt that his decision to withdraw was its main focus. Nineteen witnesses were called, including Carr himself, who had now returned to his battalion. In his statement to the court, Carr indicated that he received no instructions from any higher authority while on the Blue Line and that he gave no orders to fall back beyond the Red Line but merely to reorganise at a position just to the rear of the Blue Line. While the majority of witnesses agreed that the brigade was in an untenable position and that Carr's decision to withdraw from the Blue Line was justified, this did not protect him from further criticism. The court of inquiry found that Carr should have taken further steps to ascertain the views of Lieutenant Colonel Milne before considering a withdrawal and that his issuing of the warning order to prepare to withdraw was a grave error. However, the court dispelled any doubts about Carr's personal courage, the author of its final report writing: 'I think that up to the point of the retirement Major CARR'S work was excellent, and he certainly showed considerable courage, endurance and good control during the advance.'

Major Carr did not bear all of the criticism. Lieutenant Colonel Milne was also censured for not gaining control of the retreating troops and ensuring that Carr received definitive instructions. The court also noted that, given the difficulties in which Carr found himself, either Major McDowell (35th Battalion) or Major Fry (34th Battalion) should have moved forward to take charge of the situation.

THE EVENING OF 12 OCTOBER 1917

With the New Zealand Division still at the German barbed wire and the brigades of the 3rd Division back at their respective start lines, the last act in the evolving defeat was the withdrawal of the 4th Australian Division. At 3.00pm the 4th Division was subjected to the first of two German counter-attacks. While these attacks were beaten back, with the retirement of the 3rd Division on its left flank, the 4th Division had no option other than withdrawal. By dark both Australian brigades were back at their respective start lines. Unknown to all however, a small group of men from the 9th Brigade was still at Hillside Farm, 200 metres in front of the main brigade defensive positions.

At 5.00pm Monash was doing his best to clarify what was happening with his division. Divisional and brigade staff officers were sent forward to gather information on the situation and preparations were made for a defensive barrage once the dispositions of the brigades were known. By 6.00pm Monash had issued rudimentary orders for the night's defence, with the 9th Brigade to hold the line from the 10th/9th Brigade boundary to the railway line. The 10th Brigade line extended from the 10th/9th Brigade boundary to Ravebeek Creek; however with the location of the 4th Division's line still unclear, Monash instructed the 9th Brigade to make physical contact with the division. The 11th Brigade was to remain the Divisional Reserve, with two of its battalions positioned forward in close support and two battalions back. The Divisional Machine-Gun Officer was responsible for ensuring that the Vickers guns were sited for defence in depth along the whole divisional frontage and integrated with the defensive barrage.

Once the defence was consolidated the routine of post-battle administration commenced. A meal was brought forward by pack mules to battalion administrative areas (Details Camp), where parties of men from each company in the battalion would collect the rations and carry them to their comrades. This was probably the division's first cooked meal since the evening of 11 October. Individual battalions had made efforts to provide a meal at lunchtime on 12 October and battalion cooks had arrived at their respective Details Camp around midday, only to be sent back as the ground conditions and fighting made any attempt to set up even a rudimentary field kitchen impossible. At the same time as rations were being delivered, ammunition resupply continued, brought forward by the brigade carrying parties to replenish the small arms munitions already expended. In the 10th Brigade, first line ammunition holdings for an infantry soldier comprised at least 170 rounds and two Mills bombs. Depending on the rate of expenditure and the efficiency of resupply during the battle, the small arms ammunition replenishment task could have been considerable.

While a hot meal and ammunition resupply were important, removal of the wounded was an obvious priority. The medical units in the division comprised the 9th, 10th and 11th Field Ambulance. Troops wounded in battle were moved back to field hospitals by the field ambulances via a series of regimental aid posts (RAPs) and relay posts (where stretcher-bearers were changed) to a loading post. Each RAP had one doctor and 16 men (four Australian Army Medical Corps and 12 infantry soldiers) to act as stretcher-bearers. Across the three field ambulances within the division, 220 Medical Corps and 164 Infantry Corps soldiers were tasked as stretcher-bearers.

Stretcher-bearers resting behind a concrete German pillbox at Zonnebeke on 12 October 1917. This location is identified in the 9th Field Ambulance medical evacuation map with a large 'Z' and the identifier 'Z. station'. The soldiers in this photo are assisting members of the 9th Field Ambulance stretcher relay system. Rather than being medics from the field ambulance, who would be located at the RAP forward of this position, these soldiers are probably from the 66th British Division or infantry soldiers from the 3rd Australian Division allocated to stretcher-bearer tasks (AWM E01204).

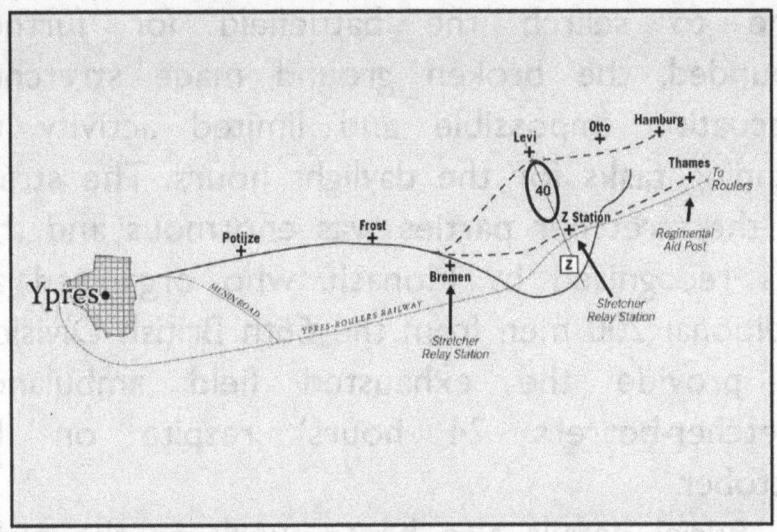

Map 14. Original map of the 9th Field Ambulance system of medical evacuation showing the RAPs and relay stations in support of the 9th Infantry Brigade on 12 October 1917.

These stretcher-bearers were heavily tasked even before the battle commenced, and during the division's approach march some 123 stretcher cases were evacuated, around 87 of these soldiers of the 66th British Division. As a result of having to clear the wounded from the 9 October battle, many of the 3rd Australian Division RAPs forward of the Red Line were undermanned on 12 October. During the course of the day, casualty rates were such that an additional 60 infantry soldier were allocated as stretcher-bearers and, by evening, some 487 stretcher cases had been carried to the rear. While nightfall would have seemed the perfect time to search the battlefield for further wounded, the broken ground made stretcher evacuation impossible and limited activity to planning tasks for the daylight hours. The strain on the stretcher parties was enormous and this was recognised by Monash, who organised an additional 200 men from the 66th British Division to provide the exhausted field ambulance stretcher-bearers 24 hours' respite on 13 October.

Burial details also began work on the night of 12 October, as the impact on morale of leaving dead comrades on the battlefield was obvious. Due to the shortage of Australian infantry, British troops were again allocated to collect the dead and 100 men from the 66th Division were given this ghastly duty. The task confronting the burial parties was daunting. An eyewitness from the 3rd Australian Division Salvage Company reported on the state of the battlefield in the Australian and New Zealand Division areas:

> ...the horrors apparent to the eye had never been seen before; men's arms, legs, and heads protruded through the mud; skeletons here and there, bodies strewing the battlefield unburied and untouched, it being impossible to bury the dead owing to

the shortage of manpower and the impossible conditions.

The Burial Section of the 3rd Australian Division interred some 253 bodies over the period from 12 to 13 October, performing this task while under artillery fire. While reports suggested that the British burial details did not complete this job as expeditiously as the Australians, it is also likely that the Australian division vacated the battlefield with many of its dead still unrecovered, despite the efforts of the Burial Section. This assertion is based in the observation of Lieutenant General Sir Arthur Currie who, as commander of the Canadian Corps, was to take over the II ANZAC Corps area. Currie wrote on 18 October 1917: 'The battlefield looks bad. No salvaging [of equipment or stores] has been done, and very few of the dead buried, particularly on 3rd Australian Division's front.'

The reality is that, immediately after the battle, the 3rd Australian Division was in no condition to perform such tasks. Indeed, on the morning of 13 October, II ANZAC Corps Headquarters described the Australian and New Zealand Divisions as '...not equal to the task of clearing the battlefield.' Since battlefield clearance usually required some minor offensive action to clear any pockets of German infiltration, this was a fair assessment. However, this did not stop Australian stretcher parties moving out at first light on 13 October to look for wounded. These parties were initially fired on by the Germans, but in a moment of quiet humanity an observer from the 40th Battalion noted that:

> ...when the enemy saw that they [the stretcher parties] were carrying wounded he ceased firing, and sent out a party of stretcher-bearers with a Red Cross flag. Our bearers moved along with the Germans, and we showed them any of their wounded, and they pointed out ours.

HOLDING THE FRONT LINE

For Monash, the days immediately following the battle were consumed with activity and provided an increasing awareness of the magnitude of the defeat suffered by his division. The initial signals from Army and Corps Headquarters tended to downplay this defeat. At 2.55am on the morning of 13 October, Godley sent Monash the text of a signal he had received from Plumer lauding the efforts of the division:

> The army commander has desired me to express to you and your Division his appreciation of the fine work done yesterday under such arduous and trying circumstances

and to say that he fully realises how gallantly all ranks carried out their difficult task.

Godley followed this up with his own handwritten note which, along with the original text from Plumer, was promulgated to the division through a Special Order by Monash's Quartermaster General:

> To General MONASH,
> Commdg. 3rd. Aust: Div.
>
> Please convey to all ranks of your Division my high appreciation of the courage and endurance displayed by your troops during the fighting of yesterday under such adverse and arduous circumstances.
>
> I sympathise with them in their disappointment at not having gained more ground, but would like [them] to realise that the 400 prisoners taken by the Corps and the large number of the enemy killed testify to the severity of the blow dealt him.
>
> It is by such repeated blows delivered by such Troops as yours that his morale is broken and the inevitable end brought nearer.
>
> Signed ... GENERAL GODLEY.

While Godley's sentiments were undoubtedly appreciated, the fact remained that the division could not deliver a blow of any weight. Overnight manpower reports from the brigades listed their fighting strengths as: 1000 men for the 9th Brigade, 500 men for the 10th Brigade and 1100 men for the 11th Brigade. These figures did not include the 500 men in infantry working parties involved in other tasks. Thus, on the morning of 13 November the total fighting strength of the division (excluding the work parties) was 2600 men, down from a strength of 5800 men at the start of the battle. With only 500 men in the 10th Brigade, this formation would be considered non-effective, leaving the division with one non-effective brigade, one fatigued and under-strength brigade (9th Brigade) and only the 11th Brigade fit for the task of holding the divisional line.

Three days after the battle (15 October 1917), burial parties of English soldiers from the 66th British Division continue to search for and inter the Australian dead (AWM E01042).

Godley would have known that a number of German prisoners had been captured (the actual number was 302 prisoners along with 11 machine-guns), but his assertion that a large number of Germans were killed during the battle was based on pure speculation. Monash, who was much closer to the action, knew so little about the course of the battle that at 9.18am on the morning of 13 October he wrote to Rosenthal trying to verify reports from Milne that the Blue Line had been reached and, if this was not the case, '...what was [the] foremost line actually reached. Also reasons for withdrawing if any...'

Despite the incomplete picture before him, the responsibilities of corps command required Godley to begin considering the next engagement. He wrote to Plumer on 13 October with an outline plan for a renewal of the attack on Passchendaele. He emphasised the need for reorganisation, noting that it would be impossible for him to renew the attack in less than a week with a preference for 10 days, to allow him to complete the reorganisation. Godley stressed the need for a heavy and deliberate bombardment to ensure any certainty of success and also '...in order to ensure success in the attack on the remainder of the Ridge, the direction of my attack should be more pivoting on my right...' This was an assessment that Godley would have done well to make before the battle, but at least he recognised the now parlous state of the New Zealand and the Australian divisions:

> The task for the 3rd Australia and New Zealand Divisions [in any future attack] is as much as they will be able to do. The troops of both are exhausted ... in the case of the 3rd Australians, not many reinforcements will be forthcoming ... and the capture of the BELLEVUE Spur is, I think, one which will need all the resources of a good Division.

Any renewed attack would be conducted by the 49th and 66th British divisions, taking a limited objective, with the requirement for a new division allocated to the corps to actually capture Passchendaele. Godley believed that the New Zealand Division could be used for any exploitation following the next battle, but made no reference to the future use of the 3rd Australian Division, presumably because the lack of reinforcements meant that it would no longer be an effective organisation.

With Godley having no immediate plans for the division it was only a matter of time before it was withdrawn from defence of the front line if for no other reason than it was barely capable of performing even this task. Correspondence from the battalion commanders of the 9th Brigade to Rosenthal, which Rosenthal then forwarded to Monash, provides an indication of the condition of the troops:

> All ranks are thoroughly fatigued and wet to the skin. They are covered in mud, and the cold and wet nights have greatly decreased their vitality.... These men were exposed since the evening 9 Oct 10th/11th when we bivouacked in the field. There was not a single tent for the battalion. The approach march and subsequent operation have so exhausted the men they are of little value as a fighting force. It would be most unwise to put such men in the line. As supporting troops they are of little use. Their condition is such that I strongly recommend immediate relief. [Lieutenant Colonel Leslie Morshead, Commanding Officer 33rd Battalion, 14 October 1917]
>
> Physically the men are done and cannot carry on. If necessary they will return to the line, but will be absolutely useless for fighting. Rifles, Lewis guns and ammunition are filled with mud and although every effort is made to clean up, the general condition of the ground makes it impossible to get the equipment in fighting order ... I would

submit the urgent necessity of relief for your consideration. [Lieutenant Colonel Ernst Martin, Commanding Officer 34th Battalion, 14 October 1917]

I have to report that the men of this Battalion are positively worn out and are unfit for further action. The rest that they are presently having on Hill 40 will not improve their condition sufficiently to make them fit even for defensive action. [Major Dowell for Commanding Officer 35th Battalion, 14 October 1917]

I am reorganising the Battalion into one Company and trying to pick up stragglers from rear areas. The condition of this battalion is as follows. They are completely worn out—many badly shaken by shelling ... [Lieutenant Colonel John Milne, Commanding Officer 36th Battalion, 14 October 1917]

The staff note from the 10th Brigade to Monash on 14 October was brief and did not contain the handwritten notes from the battalion commanders that Rosenthal had included.

However, the picture being painted was the same:

37th BATTALION. 427 went over. 290 estimated casualties, including 11 Officer casualties (1 Officer killed)...

38th BATTALION. 600 went over (including 1 company of 39th Battalion). Unable to estimate casualties...

39th BATTALION. 450 went over. 250 estimated casualties. Lost between 30 and 40 during approach march...

40th BATTALION. 450 went over. Estimated casualties not available...

To stiffen the Australian and New Zealand positions, on 13 October Godley directed that the Reserve Brigades of the 49th and 66th British divisions be placed at the disposal of Monash and Russell, with the 147th Brigade allocated to the New Zealanders and the 198th Brigade to the Australians. Bolstered by these reinforcements, both divisions would remain in the line until II ANZAC Corps was relieved by the Canadian Corps, with the latter expected to resume the offensive against Passchendaele in the near future.

Surviving soldiers of the 10th Brigade attempt to dry their clothing as they rest after the battle (AWM E00943).

By the morning of 14 October the Australian line was being held by the 11th Brigade which had taken over on the night of 13/14 October. The survivors from the 9th and 10th brigades were resting in their respective brigade support areas, behind the 11th Brigade. With the decision that the Australians would hold the line until relieved by the Canadians, these survivors now faced a return to the front line. Before they did so, the Australian division was further reinforced by the 148th Brigade, also from the 49th British Division, which replaced the 10th Brigade. The 10th Brigade was withdrawn and sent to a rest area at Bléquin in the Pas-de-Calais area of northern France. This would give Monash command of the British 198th and 148th brigades and the 9th and 11th Australian brigades which held his front line.

THE BRITISH SMALL BOX RESPIRATOR

Germany deployed 57,000 tons of poison gas during the war, primarily delivered through 33 million gas shells. It produced irritant gases such as 'sneezing' gas, 'tear' gas and more lethal 'blistering' agents such as mustard gas. Mustard gas was produced in the greatest quantity, since mustard gas shells proved to be twice as effective as the average gas shell and almost five times as effective as high explosive shells. These gases were often used in combinations with the irritation and vomiting of the 'sneezing' and 'tear' gas causing soldiers to remove their gas masks, making then susceptible to 'blistering' or mustard gas that attacked the skin and caused damage to the eyes, throat and lungs. Poison gas could be delivered in a variety of methods including in shells, aerial bombs or borne on the wind once released from static cylinders. By 1916 the BEF had introduced into service the most effective gas mask produced during the war in the form of the Small Box Respirator. The Small Box

Respirator consisted of a rubberised face mask with a fabric-covered rubber hose fitting into a chemical-absorbent canister containing charcoal and soda lime in layers of cotton pads. The provision of a nose clip and an internal mouthpiece meant that the mask did not have to have an airtight fitting for protection from 'sneezing' gas. The widespread use of the Small Box Respirator meant that German gas attacks against protected troops were rarely lethal, but saturating areas such as gun positions with mustard gas could make them uninhabitable for some time. By far the greatest impact of a gas attack was a reduction in unit efficiency, particularly when moving at night, since it impaired soldiers' vision and inhibited their breathing.

Soldiers of the 45th Battalion, 12th Brigade, 4th Australian Division, wearing Small Box Respirators near Menin Road, Ypres, 27 September 1917 (AWM E00825).

Over the following days there was an elaborate but successful orchestration of troop movements to effect these changes. The 9th Brigade relieved the 11th Brigade in the front line on the night of 15/16 October, but not before 9th Brigade Headquarters was gassed by German shells. German shelling of the Second Army rear areas was particularly frequent during the period 14—19 October, with German artillery using a combination of high explosive and poison gases.

Gas attacks notwithstanding, officers from the 148th Brigade arrived at 9th Brigade

Headquarters on the afternoon of 16 October to discuss dispositions for the relief of the brigade. Until this was completed however, the 9th Brigade was responsible for holding the entire divisional front with only the 11th Brigade in support. By the morning of 14 October the 11th Brigade had relieved the 10th Brigade, which prepared to move to Bléquin by bus the next day.

With no firm date fixed for the relief of the 9th Brigade (the night of 17/18 October was the interim date) by the 148th Brigade, Monash had to prepare a plan for the defence of his division's part of the front line. A provisional scheme for defence of the divisional area was released on 16 October. This scheme saw three brigades defending the front line in echelon, named the 'Front Line Brigade', the 'Supporting Brigade' and the 'Reserve Brigade' respectively. The total frontage to be held was roughly 1300 metres, but the defended portion was only 900 metres since the undefended area around Ravebeek Creek was regarded as so boggy that a German attack at night through the area was deemed impossible. Further, it was assessed that if the Germans attacked by day through this area they would be fired on from the higher ground near the Ypres—Roulers railway line, creating a reverse Bellevue spur situation—but only if this higher ground was held. The 'Front Line Brigade' was permitted to keep the eight Vickers machine-guns of its machine-gun company for direct fire purposes, but the rest of the divisional machine-guns would be allocated to either rest or barrage work.

The 9th Brigade settled into a routine of defence works and night patrolling, although these requirements would prove short-lived. The brigade was officially relived by the 148th Brigade at 10.30pm on 18 October, the troops moving out of the line and marching to Campagne lès Boulonnais, also in the Pas-de-Calais area. The 11th Brigade was to remain in the divisional area in the 'Supporting Brigade' role until 22 October, when it would be relieved by the Canadian 50th Battalion. The brigade then moved by a combination of bus and train to join its two sister brigades in the Bléquin/Campagne lés Boulonnais area, formally ending the 3rd Australian Division's involvement in the Passchendaele battle.

CHAPTER 6

PASSCHENDAELE II: THE CANADIAN CORPS ATTACK

On 13 October, the morning after the failed II ANZAC Corps attack, Haig held a conference with Plumer and Gough at Second Army Headquarters. During the meeting he reiterated to both that his aim to capture Passchendaele had not changed and that the '...immediate objective was the mass of high ground about Passchendaele. Once this was taken the rest of the ridge would fall more easily.' Haig was well acquainted with the problems caused by the rain and mud and their impact on lines of communication in the previous battle as he had received regular updates on the condition of the battlefield. It was agreed that a respite of 10 to 12 days and, importantly, a period of fine weather, would be required before any new attack could be launched. Haig's larger operational-level imperatives associated with keeping the German Army focused on Flanders remained, even if his tactical focus had now narrowed to the sole aim of capturing the main ridge north to Westroosebeke in order to provide the BEF a favourable winter position.

The Canadian Corps, which had last seen intensive action in August at Lens-Vimy, was selected to replace II ANZAC Corps and continue the attack, and Canadian Corps commander Lieutenant General Arthur Currie was directed to submit an appropriate plan to Haig. Currie had no objection to the operation, but preferred to have the Canadian Corps serve under Plumer rather than Gough since he had doubts over the latter's ability. The Canadian *Official History* suggests that Haig's own Chief of Staff, Lieutenant General Sir Launcelot Kiggell, recognised Currie's reluctance to work under Gough and arranged the corps transfer to Plumer without an official request from Currie. Regardless of how it occurred, this preference was accommodated and the Canadians would attack Passchendaele under command of Second Army rather than Fifth Army, setting the scene for attacks by the Canadian Corps over the period 26 October to 10 November. A brief examination of these attacks is warranted, if only because their ultimate success serves to illuminate some of the reasons II ANZAC Corps and the 3rd Australian Division failed to achieve the same outcome.

THE ATTACKS: 26 OCTOBER TO 10 NOVEMBER

Currie's plan involved three staged attacks, with objectives that roughly corresponded to the Australian Red, Blue and Green lines. But Currie's plan was far less ambitious than that of the Australians. In a classic application of 'bite and hold' tactics, the attack on each line would be punctuated by intervals of three to four days to enable artillery and fresh troops to be brought forward for the subsequent attack. At a conference on 16 October, Currie made it clear that the date for the first attack would depend on adequate artillery preparation, which in turn required a substantial improvement in the state of the roads. This could not be achieved without a period of fine weather to firm the ground. Currie correctly appreciated that, without these preconditions being met, the preparatory barrage would not cut the German barbed wire or neutralise their defences.

The Canadian approach to battle had been built on carefully planned set-piece engagements and their processes had been refined during their battles at Vimy Ridge and Hill 70 at Lens. An effective artillery barrage was an essential element of Currie's battle plan for Passchendaele and he was determined to achieve this. Since he would take over the Australian artillery for the attack, Currie sent his GOC Royal Artillery, Brigadier Edward Morrison, to conduct a personal inspection of the Australian guns and their associated positions. Morrison later professed to have experienced 'a rude awakening', assessing the condition of the Australian artillery as lamentable. Of the 250 heavy artillery pieces supposed to be in the corps area, he could find only 227, of which 89 were unserviceable. The field artillery was in a worse condition. Of the 306 18-pounders on strength, less than half were capable of action. The disabled guns had remained *in situ* on the battlefield, since the Australians had decided not to return them to the rear in order to keep roads open. Due to the shortage of firm ground, the disposition of the artillery was also poor, the guns arrayed in four clusters, allowing the Germans to maximise the effectiveness of their counter-battery fire.

The Canadian Corps also organised their artillery in a different manner to the rest of the BEF. In Canadian doctrine, 'corps control' of artillery took priority in the planning and conduct of a battle. This control encompassed all artillery assets participating in the battle from whatever source. The next phase was 'divisional control', which only resumed once the battle was over.

Finally, 'normal control' occurred when operations along the front line were static. Thus Currie had direct control of all artillery assets assigned to his corps for the conduct of the forthcoming battle, a far more favourable situation than that enjoyed by the remainder of the BEF in which artillery control between army, corps and divisional assets was not as well defined. These clear lines of operational and technical control ensured that the Canadian artillery was effectively utilised and, over the course of the Passchendaele battles, Canadian gunners were to fire 1,453,056 shells of all calibres.

LIEUTENANT GENERAL SIR ARTHUR WILLIAM CURRIE, GCMG, KCB

Arthur Currie was born in Adelaide Township in Ontario, Canada, in 1875 to poor Irish immigrants. He grew up in a strict, religious household and trained to be a teacher, but later became an insurance salesman and failed real estate investor. He joined a local militia in 1897 as a gunner in the No.5 (British Columbia) Garrison Artillery. He rose rapidly through the ranks and by 1909 was commanding the unit with the rank of lieutenant colonel. In 1914 he took charge of the newly raised 50th Regiment, Gordon

Highlanders of Canada, and was involved in a financial irregularity that saw him use CA$10,833 of regimental funds to pay off his personal debts. It would be almost three years before this money was repaid to the regiment with funds borrowed from two of Currie's subordinates. With the outbreak of war Currie accepted command of one of the four infantry brigades in the Canadian Expeditionary Force. For his leadership of the 2nd Canadian Brigade during Second Ypres, Currie was promoted and given command of the 1st Canadian Division. A believer in detailed staff work and training, Currie's career was ascending and in June 1917 he was given command of the Canadian Corps which he retained until the end of the war. Currie returned to Canada in August 1919, was appointed Inspector-General of the Canadian Armed Forces and promoted to full general. However, he baulked at implementing his government-mandated task of cost cutting, preferring to retire from the military in 1920 before accepting the position of Vice-Chancellor of McGill University in Montreal. Despite the financial restrictions of the Great Depression Currie established a number of new departments within the university and also served as President of the

National Conference of Canadian Universities from 1925 to 1927. He was forced to defend his wartime reputation in a libel suit against a national newspaper, winning the case but receiving little compensation. Currie was elected Dominion President of the Canadian Legion of the British Empire Service League in 1928, but suffered a stroke the following year. He died in 1933 at the age of 57 and was buried in Montreal following a state funeral.

Lieutenant General Sir Arthur Currie as commander of he Canadian Corps in 1917 (AWM 1106979).

Canadian soldiers moving past the ruined Cloth Hall in Ypres on their way to the front on 25 October 1917. Given that the first Canadian attack was to occur the next day, these troops were possibly designated for one of the later attacks (AWM E04715).

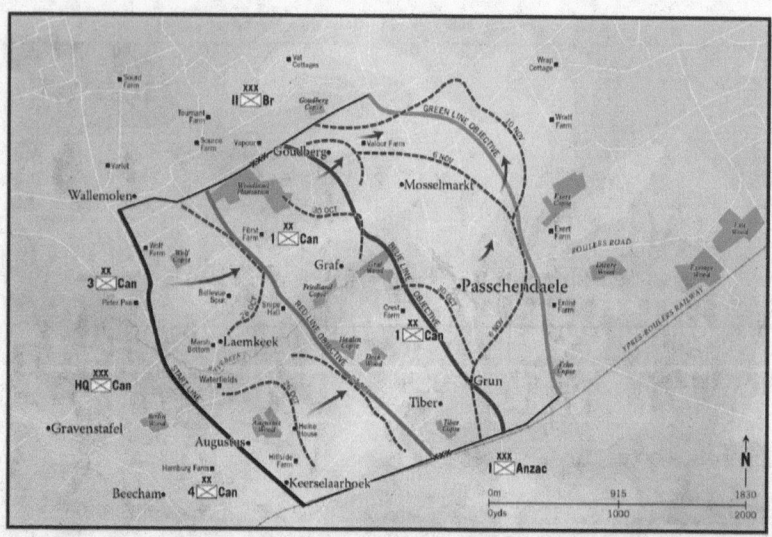

Map 15. The Canadian attacks on Passchendaele from 26 October to 10 November 1917. Unlike the II ANZAC Corps plan to capture the Red, Blue and Green Line objectives in one day, Currie's plan set these as objectives for individual attacks spread over a number of days (26 October, 30 October, 6 November and 10 November).

Fortunately, by mid-October the weather had indeed improved and, despite continuous German artillery fire, considerable progress had been made in the construction of plank roads within the corps area. While the Canadian Corps suffered some 1500 casualties during these logistic preparations, Currie pushed on, recognising the essential nature of these works. The Canadians also benefited from the discovery that, beneath a deep covering of mud, the base of the Frezenberg—Zonnebeke road remained intact, providing an additional circuit for the movement of guns and supplies. Given these advantages Morrison managed to push three brigades of field artillery forward, bring up additional heavy guns to perform counter-battery work and stockpile munitions for the coming attack.

An aerial view of Passchendaele village on 17 October 1917. The road leading into the village is most likely the Ypres—Zonnebeke—Broodseinde—Passchendaele road which follows the high ground of Passchendaele Ridge, the route taken by the Canadian 10th Brigade (AWM J00285).

Currie's appreciation of the terrain and how it could be used differed from Monash's. In planning the attack Currie decided to use one brigade (Canadian 10th Brigade from the 4th Canadian Division) in the area where Monash had employed two (Australian 9th and 10th brigades). This gave the Canadian 10th Brigade space to manoeuvre and, by moving up the firmer ground along Passchendaele Ridge, it avoided the swampy ground close to Ravebeek Creek. The Australian 9th Brigade had taken a similar route, but had been constrained to some degree by the need to maintain contact with the Australian 10th Brigade on its left flank, which had faced the double impediment of German fire from the Bellevue spur as well as the hard going close to Ravebeek Creek. Currie recognised that Ravebeek Creek, while negotiable by small parties of men, was impassable to any formation large enough to constitute a viable German counter-attack. As such, there was no need to physically protect this flank with troops. Under Currie's appreciation the entire 1200 metres of the 10th Brigade frontage could now be covered by a smaller number of troops and the brigade led the attack with one battalion. Finally, as a corps commander, Currie had an advantage over Monash in enjoying the freedom to decide the focus of his corps attack. Currie clearly understood the significance of the Bellevue spur to the capture of Passchendaele and it was here he would place his main effort.

THE ATTACK OF 26 OCTOBER 1917

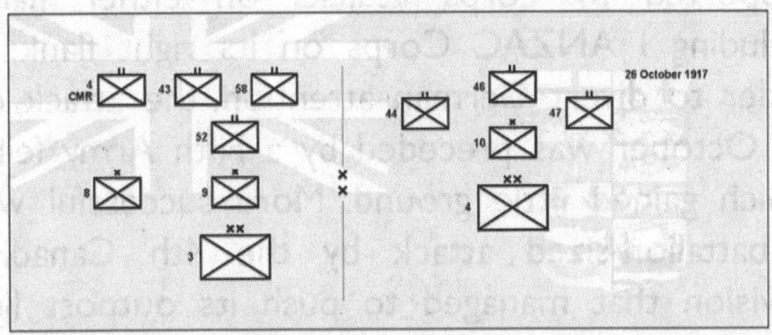

Diagram 8. The Canadian Corps attack formation, 26 October 1917.

Currie was fortunate in that he could choose the timing of his battle, with Haig impressing on Plumer that the Canadians were not required to begin the attack until they were ready to do so. Given the prospect of reasonable weather, Currie had selected the morning of 26 October as a suitable date. The attack would be made with two divisions, the corps boundaries essentially the same as those employed by II ANZAC Corps. Within the Canadian Corps area the divisional boundary (as with the New Zealand and 3rd Australian divisions) was along Ravebeek Creek. On the right the 4th Canadian Division would attack with one brigade (10th Brigade), with one battalion leading and two battalions in support. On the left the 3rd Canadian Division would attack the Bellevue spur with two brigades (8th and 9th brigades) across a three-battalion frontage. The Canadian Corps would be supported by corps attacks on either flank, including I ANZAC Corps on its right flank. In order to divert German attention, the attack on 26 October was preceded by a Fifth Army feint, which gained little ground. More successful was a battalion-sized attack by the 4th Canadian Division that managed to push its outpost line some 250 to 350 metres up Passchendaele Ridge.

The attack on the morning of 26 October was launched in heavy rain, which had commenced around midnight. On the right, the lead battalion of the Canadian 10th Brigade (the 46th Battalion) advanced some 350 metres and achieved its first objective. Consolidating on the position, the men were subjected to heavy German fire from Passchendaele. This fire supported a series of German counter-attacks that almost drove the battalion back to its start line and the situation was only retrieved when two supporting battalions assisted the 46th Battalion to regain its objective.

On the left the Allied artillery barrage had broken the German wire in front of the Bellevue spur and the three leading battalions of the 3rd Canadian Division, unlike the New Zealand Division, were able to make rapid progress through this obstacle. The 43rd (Cameron Highlanders of Canada) Battalion managed to penetrate the German pillboxes and establish a precarious position which was still some 400 yards short of its objective. Isolated and under intense fire, the 43rd Battalion was reduced to just 50 men. The 52nd Battalion (Manitoba) was sent to reinforce these survivors and, taking advantage of the easier movement through the sandy soil on top of the spur, managed to outflank the German pillboxes on Bellevue. By 3.30pm the assaulting battalions had largely driven the Germans from their Bellevue spur positions in the Flanders I defence line and, while the Canadians were short of their objective on their left flank, this failure was not decisive. The first stage of Currie's advance had been a success and the Canadian Corps was now firmly established on Passchendaele Ridge with a crucial foothold on the Bellevue spur.

In the four days following the first attack the Canadians made strenuous efforts to improve their lines of communication and replenish artillery munitions. Main roads were repaired with the bricks and rubble from ruined villages, while each brigade constructed a track network from its forward lines back to brigade headquarters using planks or fascines. Munitions for the field artillery were brought forward to the gun lines by trains of pack animals, replenished from the main ammunition dumps at Frezenberg and Wieltje, north-east of Ypres. By this time, light rail was also being extended in the corps area and provided a practical means for replenishing the heavy artillery. All these tasks were performed under German artillery fire, complemented by intense air activity, ensuring that the Canadians suffered significant casualties.

THE ATTACK OF 30 OCTOBER 1917

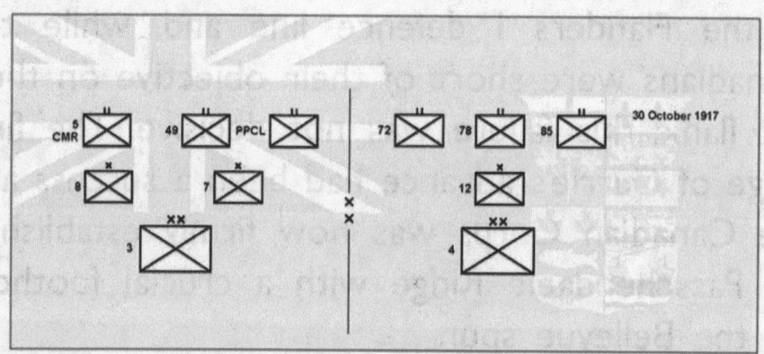

Diagram 9. The Canadian Corps attack formation, 30 October 1917.

The attack on 30 October had three objectives. On the right flank, the 4th Canadian Division would advance 600 metres to outflank the German pillbox complex at Crest Farm, the very complex which would have blocked any attempt by the Australian 10th Brigade to advance up the Ravebeek Creek re-entrant. On the left flank the 3rd Canadian Division would advance 700 metres to capture the German positions near Meetcheele, the objective it had failed to achieve on 26 October. Once Meetcheele was secured, the division would then advance another 450 metres, clearing German positions to the approaches of Passchendaele along the entire Bellevue—Meetcheele ridge.

At 5.50am the Canadian attack commenced in fine weather, but with a strong and cold wind. On the right, the 12th Brigade of the 4th Canadian Division secured Crest Farm and reached the outskirts of Passchendaele. The Canadians achieved this despite taking heavy casualties from those remaining German positions on the Bellevue—Meetcheele ridge, their experience similar to that of the Australian 9th Brigade. On the left, the attack was not proceeding as well for the 3rd Canadian Division which was now engaged in heavy fighting along the summit of the Bellevue spur. While the two battalions of the 7th Brigade made minimal progress, the lone battalion of the 8th Brigade (5th Canadian Mounted Rifles) battled along the northern edge of the Bellevue spur. Traversing swampy ground with both flanks exposed, the battalion seized a number of farmhouses north-east of Passchendaele which it then held, despite being reduced to just 40 men. Desperate to restore their position on the Bellevue spur, the Germans launched no fewer than five counter-attacks during the course of the afternoon, all of which were beaten back.

Despite the limited progress along the ridge of the Bellevue spur, the German Flanders II defence line had been substantially breached, with only the immediate defences of Passchendaele itself now standing between the Canadians and victory. It was a measure of the intensity of the fighting that, over the two attacks, seven Victoria Crosses were awarded to the soldiers of the two Canadian divisions. While this attack did not mark the end of the German defence system (the German Flanders III defence line still ran parallel to Passchendaele and Westroosebeke villages), the impending capture of both villages and their associated ridge would soon place the German Army in the unaccustomed position of having its defences overlooked by Allied forces.

THE ATTACK OF 6 NOVEMBER 1917

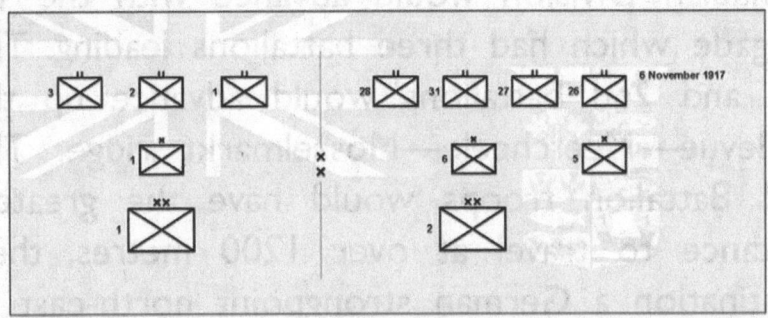

Diagram 10. The Canadian Corps attack formation, 6 November 1917.

The objective for the Canadian attack on 6 November was the old Australian Green Line, which covered an arc east and north-east of Passchendaele. This attack would be conducted by two fresh divisions from within the Canadian Corps and, by 5 November, the 1st and 2nd Canadian divisions had relieved the 3rd and 4th Canadian divisions. During the period 1 to 4 November, just prior to the main attack, a number of smaller preliminary operations were completed to improve the Canadian start-line positions.

For the main attack, Currie placed the 2nd Canadian Division on the right, with two brigades leading on a four-battalion frontage. Three battalions, the 28th, 31st and 27th battalions from the 6th Brigade, would capture Passchendaele, with a further battalion from the 5th Brigade providing flank protection. On the left, the 1st Canadian Division would advance with the 1st Brigade which had three battalions leading. The 1st and 2nd battalions would advance up the Bellevue—Meetcheele—Mosselmarkt ridge. The 3rd Battalion troops would have the greatest distance to travel at over 1200 metres, their destination a German strongpoint north-east of Passchendaele.

The attack commenced at 6.00am in cold, rainy weather. On the right, now well up the ridge, the ground traversed by the 2nd Canadian Division was dry and firm. With favourable ground conditions the Canadians moved so quickly that the German defensive barrage largely fell behind the advancing troops. Closely following their own Allied barrage, the Canadians were often on top of the German troops before they could man their machineguns. By 7.10am the advance had captured the village and was pushing beyond to its Green Line objective, which was secured by 8.45am. On the left the 1st Canadian Division had to advance on the narrow 350-metre Bellevue—Meetcheele ridge, the top of which held the only firm ground. Despite stiff German resistance, by 8.00am the 1st Canadian Division had also reached its Green Line.

Passchendaele and its immediate environs had been captured.

THE ATTACK OF 10 NOVEMBER 1917

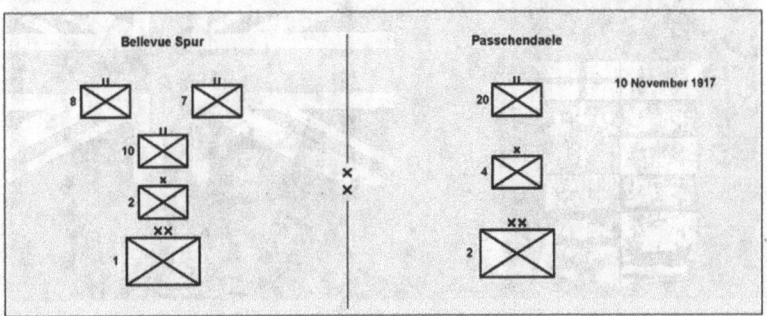

Diagram 11. The Canadian Corps attack formation, 10 November 1917.

On 7 November Currie issued his orders for the final Canadian attack. The objective was the ground around the Vindictive Crossroads, the highest point on the northern end of Passchendaele Ridge, and some 1000 yards to the north of Passchendaele. Once this was secure, the Allies would dominate German defences to the north and the north-east. The main thrust of the attack would be conducted on the left by the 2nd Brigade of the 1st Canadian Division, with two battalions leading. On the right, the 4th Brigade would provide flanking support with one battalion.

Canada Gate, located at the edge of Crest Farm on what is now the western edge of Passchendaele village. Dedicated in November 2017, the gate commemorates 100 years since the successful conclusion of the battle for Passchendaele by the Canadian Corps on 10 November 1917 (image courtesy of Bill Frost).

The 1st Division frontage for the attack was narrow and it was raining heavily when the attack commenced just after 6.00am. By 7.30am, following an advance of some 450 metres, the 7th and 8th battalions had secured their objectives. The 10th Battalion then passed through these two forward battalions to continue the attack. However the attack by the British division on the left flank of the 1st Division stalled, resulting in a further contraction of the

Canadian front. This narrow frontage allowed the German defensive batteries to concentrate their fire, inflicting a number of casualties. In the afternoon the Germans launched two counter-attacks, but the Canadians managed to hold onto their gains down the eastern slopes of the ridge.

This final Canadian attack on 10 November represented the end of the battle for Passchendaele and brought the Third Ypres campaign to a conclusion. In 16 days the Canadian Corps had fought four set-piece battles and a number of battalion-sized preliminary operations. The Corps took over 1200 German prisoners, but suffered 12,924 casualties in the process, of whom 4028 were killed in action. The Canadian Corps made significant advances up Passchendaele Ridge, but did not accomplish Haig's intent of capturing the entire main ridge north to Westroosebeke.

CHAPTER 7

CONCLUSION: THE 3RD AUSTRALIAN DIVISION AT PASSCHENDAELE I

THE CONTROVERSY

Passchendaele remains a contentious battle on many levels. The first issue is the degrading of Haig's operational aims. The Third Ypres campaign commenced with ambitious operational objectives and concluded in a tactical battle in which attrition and the ability to achieve limited objectives became the measure of success. Loss of operational aims during the course of a campaign is a common occurrence and one of the skills of generalship is the ability to assess when the costs of continuing a campaign outweigh the benefits. In this regard, the question to be asked was whether Haig's broader operational aims could still be achieved by fighting the Passchendaele battle. To Haig's critics the battle was pointless and the casualties suffered cannot be justified since the original intent was no longer achievable. Haig's supporters however, while acknowledging that his original operational aims had changed significantly, argue that the battle played a valuable role in eroding German strength on the Western Front.

The second controversial issue linked to Passchendaele concerns the conditions in which the battle was fought. Images of soldiers and horses struggling through the muddy morass of the Ypres salient have become a post-war metaphor for both the horrors of the First World War and the failure of BEF leadership. However, such sentiments do not assist an objective assessment of the impact of mud and rain on the course of the battle. Soldiering in difficult conditions is not a new phenomenon and there are very few terrain types and conditions in which infantry soldiers cannot operate—the question is one of degree. At Passchendaele, small groups such as platoons successfully navigated the difficult ground of Ravebeek Creek, while larger formations such as battalions soon lost cohesion in attempting the same task. While all of the approaches to Passchendaele were difficult, the terrain was not impassable, particularly the relatively firmer and drier ground on the Bellevue and Passchendaele ridges. This meant that the ground suitable for a successful infantry approach to Passchendaele was significantly restricted, a fact not lost on the German Army in the siting of its defensive positions. Of equal importance was the impact of mud on the artillery placement, movement, resupply and effectiveness. Given the central role of the barrage in the BEF's design for battle in 1917 any restrictions on a barrage due to environmental conditions could have enormous consequences.

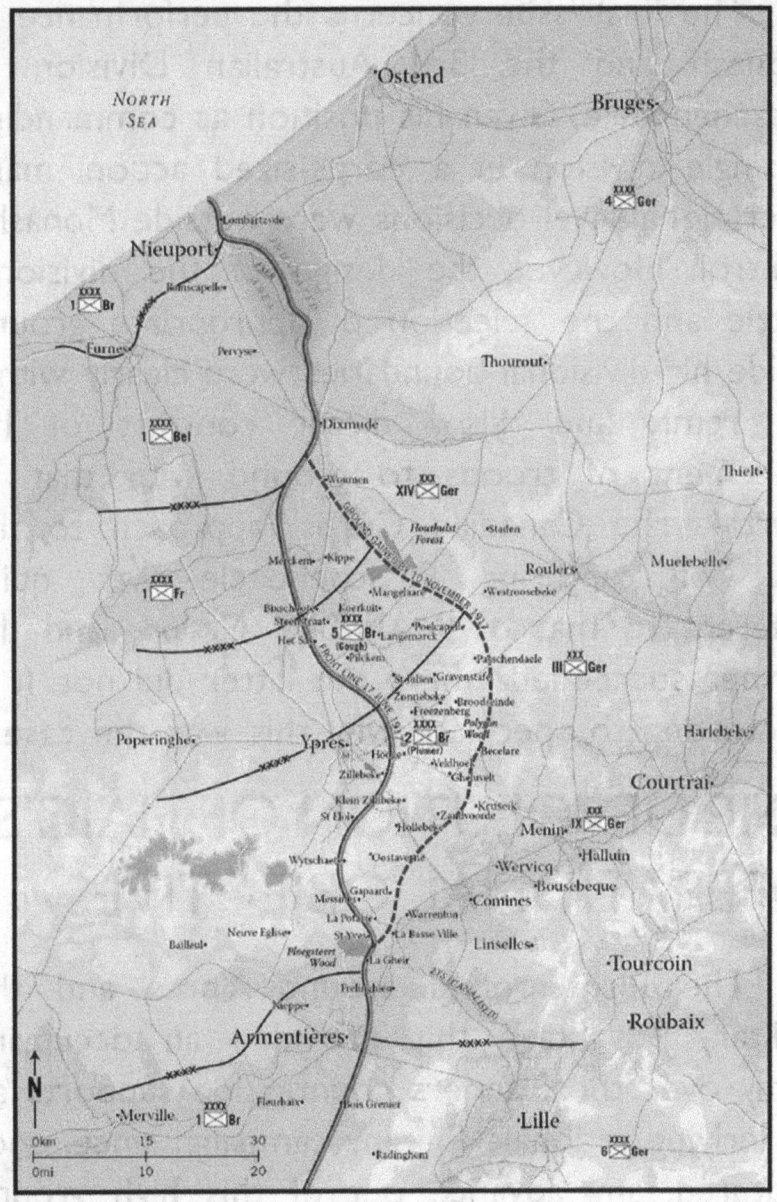

Map 16. The extent of the Allied advance in the Third Ypres campaign, commencing with the Battle of Messines on 17 June 1917 and concluding with the attack by the Canadian Corps on 10 November 1917. The British Official History lists Allied casualties of all types during the campaign as 262,875 and German casualties an estimated 423,000.

The final issue concerns the performance of Monash and the 3rd Australian Division at Passchendaele. Given his position as commanding a single division in a corps-sized action, many operational-level decisions were outside Monash's control. However, the design of the divisional battle and the selection of appropriate ground inside his divisional boundaries were clearly within his remit and allow direct contrast of his placement of troops to ground with that of Currie. The Canadian Corps' approach to the task of capturing Passchendaele was quite different to that of II ANZAC Corps—and the former succeeded where the latter did not. It is interesting to speculate why this was the case.

THE DEVOLUTION OF HAIG'S OPERATIONAL OBJECTIVES

The high ground around Ypres and the military advantage this provided an occupying army over the Flanders countryside supports an underlying rationale for any campaign since, once captured, any advance out of this high ground offered the Allies a number of operational opportunities. One of these opportunities included a 1916 Admiralty plan to advance north-east and capture the channel ports which supported German submarine operations. For reasons which were possibly based on his First Ypres campaign experience, Haig was predisposed to support the Admiralty position. This was reinforced in the June 1917 meeting of the Cabinet Committee on War Policy when the First Sea Lord asserted that, should Haig not take the channel ports, Britain would be unable to continue the war into 1918. Subsequent events were to weaken the validity of the Admiralty assessment since it was the introduction of a new naval tactic in the form of the convoy system in May 1917, just prior to the commencement of Haig's campaign, which was to ease the U-boat threat.

Admiralty logic for the capture of the channel ports did not invalidate Haig's assessment that the Western Front was the decisive theatre of the war. In early 1917, when David Lloyd George moved to divert British divisions to the Italian front, Haig successfully fought to retain the BEF in the west for the Third Ypres campaign. In this Haig had the support of the French who had suffered a number of mutinies in May and June 1917 and requested a BEF offensive to relieve pressure on their army. While this would have been a factor in Haig's decision to continue with the Ypres campaign after the Battle of Messines, it was not a decisive reason for doing so. Haig was also wary of French motives and probably recognised that, while the mutinies would affect the French Army's ability to conduct offensives, it could still hold ground.

The most convincing reason for the BEF's mounting and then continuing the Third Ypres campaign is the simplest. Both the French and British governments were eager to prosecute an offensive that would expel the German Army from French and Belgian soil and expected their military to pursue a strategy that would conclude the war rather than prolong the status quo. With the French Army exhausted by Verdun in 1916 and the failed Nivelle offensive in April-May 1917, the BEF was the only force capable of mounting an effective campaign. Failure to prosecute such an offensive would not only waste the offensive potential of the BEF, but would also allow the German Army respite to recover from its losses of 1916 and perhaps consolidate its defensive position in the west.

Once the time and location for a BEF offensive in 1917 had been decided, the question was simply how it should be conducted. Haig's plan for the campaign has been the subject of much criticism. Rather than conducting a series of 'bite and hold' battles, Haig opted for a breakout battle followed by what he hoped would be an exploitation/pursuit phase. Criticism of Haig's operational plan predicated on a breakout battle is not unjustified since Plumer's 'bite and hold' tactics represented a proven method of crossing no man's land with acceptable losses. Conversely, Gough's breakout battle carried little opportunity for success, produced heavy losses once the infantry outran their artillery support and had largely failed to produce the required results in the post-1914 battles. However, Haig also recognised the key weakness of the 'bite and hold' tactics. Limited advances of several hundred metres at a time, no matter how successful, were never going to be decisive. As the BEF commander it was his task to design campaigns that could produce decisive operational-level outcomes, as only then could results justify the attendant losses. Thus criticism of Haig's initial decision not to use 'bite and hold' tactics are somewhat ironic, since such tactics relied on achieving operational goals through the mechanism of attrition rather than manoeuvre.

The unfortunate delay between the attack at Messines on 7 June and the commencement of Gough's attack on 31 July cost Haig operational surprise and allowed the German Army an opportunity to strengthen its Flanders defence lines. Such a delay was necessary to bring forward the required artillery and munitions, but it was also a consequence of conducting the Ypres offensive from a salient. By its very nature a salient offered less room for the attacking force than would be available along a broad front. It also provided the defender the opportunity to concentrate artillery fire around the more restricted area of the salient, rather than disperse this fire over an entire front. For a BEF that was slowly pushing its way forward in the Ypres salient, the restricted ground of the salient meant that the routes and logistics needed to sustain the offensive became increasingly complex and demanding.

Following the failure of Gough's attempts to achieve a breakout in August, Haig switched the main effort of the campaign to Plumer with orders to conduct a series of 'bite and hold' battles. In early October, just prior to the Battle of Broodseinde, the weather began to deteriorate and considerable engineering effort was required just to maintain the basic road networks. The logistic demands of continuing the offensive increased significantly and the constraints on moving munitions and artillery in particular began to limit the effectiveness of attacks. The changes in operational method, combined with changes in the weather, also brought a gradual shift in Haig's objectives. As the probability of achieving his operational aims began to diminish, they were replaced by a tactical-level goal of securing a superior winter position for the BEF on top of the Passchendaele—Westroosebeke ridge.

If the Third Ypres campaign had lost its operational focus, its tactical focus was soon to follow. Once the heavy rains commenced in early October, the weather provided ample opportunity to halt the campaign. Haig elected to continue, based on a requirement to secure a winter position, but this reason no longer supported his underlying operational rationale for pursuing the campaign. Haig believed the intelligence estimates that described the German Army as close to collapse and suggested that the Passchendaele attack would precipitate this process. Once the campaign lost momentum and the amount of ground gained continued to diminish, German Army losses became a natural focus for measuring success. Shifts in German casualties and morale assumed the greatest importance as BEF intelligence became increasingly optimistic that political discord within Germany, when combined with a manpower crisis, would be reflected in a breakdown of discipline on the battlefield. By early September Haig was convinced that cumulative pressure was building on the German Army and that the quality of the German front-line divisions was in decline. Following the Broodseinde attack on 4 October Second Army intelligence noted the poor quality of the German counter-attacks and a marked deterioration in organisation and morale. While this was certainly the case, the German Army had also initiated the practice of rotating its divisions through the front line far more rapidly and for a shorter time period. The divisions Second Army faced at Broodseinde would be vastly different to those it would fight at Poelcappelle or Passchendaele I.

Critics have argued that the BEF's Chief of Intelligence, Brigadier General Charteris, was responsible for Haig's optimism, producing reports that fed Haig's desire to continue the campaign. Such a proposition overplays Charteris's role, as his intelligence reports reinforced rather than initiated Haig's decision to continue the campaign. The problem with Haig's intelligence process was that it was predicated on optimism. Beach, in his book, *Haig's Intelligence. GHQ and the German Army, 1916-1918*, notes that the very offensive mechanism of the BEF created a treadmill, with forward offensive action generating new information on German morale, which in turn generated further optimism. While the German Army was clearly under considerable stress by late 1917, it would not begin to disintegrate until the summer of 1918. Indeed a Second Army intelligence report of August 1917 paints a more accurate picture of the German Army at this stage of the war, describing the German infantry as demonstrating considerable powers of resistance despite the adverse weather, British artillery superiority, and being forced to live in shell holes instead of trenches.

With the hope of reaching the channel ports lost, a winter position for the BEF on the Passchendaele—Westroosebeke ridge became desirable rather than essential. The internal destruction of the German Army was not a possibility in 1917 and Haig's strategy of attrition was now an aspiration rather than a strategy likely to produce a decisive outcome. In such circumstances it is logical to conclude that the attack at Passchendaele was not justified since it was conducted without an achievable operational goal. Interestingly, German post-war literature infused new life into the attrition debate. Its authors supported Haig's argument that prolonging the Third Ypres campaign kept the German Army engaged in Flanders, thereby reducing the German strategic options and depleting their manpower. In May 1917, following the Battle of Arras, the Chief of Staff to the *1st Bavarian Reserve Corps* wrote:

> The wastage of manpower, such as occurred on the Somme, certainly cannot be repeated this year without seriously endangering the ability of Germany to wage war and without bringing about the exhaustion towards which the enemy is

aiming through his massive deployment of men and steel.

This 'wastage of manpower' is exactly what the Third Ypres campaign was to inflict on the German Army. General of Infantry Herman von Kuhl, Chief of Staff, *Army Group Rupprecht*, wrote after the campaign:

> It would be quite wrong to deny the British credit for the courage with which they fought and for the obstinate way they brushed aside the heaviest casualties and kept renewing their assault. It would be equally wrong to suggest that there was any possibility that they might have broken through. The fact that, despite this, they continued their offensive was justified by the British on the basis of the overall situation ... The French army gained time to recover its strength: the German reserves were drawn towards Flanders. The sacrifices that the British made for the Entente were fully justified.

But Von Kuhl's commander, Field Marshal Crown Prince Rupprecht of Bavaria, was less generous in his assessment of what the Third Ypres campaign had achieved. In December 1917 the Special Order of the Day to his Army Group stated:

Despite the deployment of immense quantities of men and material, the enemy achieved absolutely nothing. A narrow, utterly smashed strip of ground represents his entire gain. He has bought this outcome at the cost of extraordinarily heavy casualties; whereas our losses were far fewer than for any previous defensive battle. As a result the Battle of Flanders has been a serious defeat for our opponents and a great victory for us.

Even allowing for his duty to maintain morale within his armies, there was certainly no sense that Passchendaele was a major defeat for the German Army, but equally there is no doubt that it kept the German Army engaged in Flanders.

THE MUD

The heavy rains which commenced on the night of 3 October and the resulting quagmire have contributed to the public image of a campaign that should never have been fought, despite the fact that, until the Battle of Broodseinde, the BEF had achieved a high degree of success. Edmonds, in the British *Official History*, maintains that the influence of mud on the Third Ypres campaign was overstated and that winter on the Somme in 1916 produced worse conditions. Writing after the Second World War, Edmonds also made the point that armies have operated in worse conditions than Flanders and succeeded, citing the Allies in Holland in 1944-45 and Fourteenth Army in Burma in 1945. In spite of Edmonds's arguments, the influence and image of mud as the main reason for the failure at Passchendaele remains the predominant paradigm.

Writing after the battle, Haig and his associated commanders had no reason to contest this viewpoint. Both Haig and Plumer blame the failure of the 12 October Passchendaele attack on the mud: '...owing to the rain and the bad state of the ground General Plumer decided that it was best not to continue the attack on the front of his Army.' Plumer's Chief of Staff, Major General Harington, was more emphatic: 'I venture to think that if we had not been "Killed by mud" we would have taken the Passchendaele-Staden Ridge with proper preparation...' Godley, writing of the conditions in which the Passchendaele battle was fought, argued:

> None but British soldiers could have done it. A German officer prisoner brought back said, when he saw the conditions, that no troops in the world except the English would have attempted an offensive with such

roads, or lack of roads, and other communications.

In his private correspondence to his wife and daughter, Monash wrote on 18 October: 'I am inclined to believe that the plan [for the battle] was fully justified, and would have succeeded in normal weather conditions.'

While the adverse impact of the mud on the movement of infantry and the artillery bombardment is not in dispute, for Monash to blame the failure of the Passchendaele attack solely on the weather is to miss the obvious failure in planning and logic—the ground conditions were known and should have been accommodated. Bean, in his criticism of Haig clearly supports this proposition:

> He continued his offensive in weather in which the basic conditions for the step-by-step [bite and hold] method were but doubtfully secured, and where its certainty of success had vanished.

Bean then contrasts the plan for the II ANZAC Corps Passchendaele I attack with the Canadian Corps attacks at Passchendaele II: 'The extreme difficulties of attacking in the wet were this time carefully met by shortening the advances and lengthening the preparation.'

While the Canadian Corps enjoyed a period of fine weather before commencing its offensive, from the morning of 26 October the Canadian battlefield was subjected to intermittent heavy showers. Based on the Canadian descriptions and photographs of the battlefield, it is unlikely that the ground conditions were substantially better than those experienced by II ANZAC Corps. However Currie, unlike Godley, was a national commander and was able to secure the time necessary to prepare an adequate barrage. While this barrage was instrumental in ensuring the success of the attack on the Bellevue spur, Currie's plan for the battle was also based on recognition of the state of the ground. Rather than the ambitious length of advance proposed in the Red-Blue-Green lines of the II ANZAC Corps plan, Currie effectively made each of these lines the subject of a separate attack. He understood that, in the muddy conditions, both the infantry rate of advance and the time required to bring forward guns and munitions precluded any other approach. There is no doubt that the mud was a major contributor to the failure of the II ANZAC Corps attack, but as the Canadian Corps showed, planning which took account of the ground conditions would have significantly increased the chances of a successful attack.

ASSESSING THE PLAN AND THE 3RD AUSTRALIAN DIVISION'S PERFORMANCE

On 1 November 1917 Monash submitted a report to Headquarters II ANZAC Corps on lessons learned from the 12 October attack. Typical of Monash's staff work, the report was concise and detailed. In the first paragraph he made the point that the time allocated for the preparation of the operation 'was entirely insufficient'. Monash considered that this lack of preparation time affected the division's communications, headquarters placements, casualty evacuation, obstacle crossing and artillery location and resupply—in short, most of the staff elements that would ensure a successful attack. In subsequent paragraphs Monash expanded on these points, his key arguments: lack of duckboards meant that the troops arrived at their start lines already exhausted; lack of buried cable meant his brigadiers had no communications and hence little control over their battle; the barrage was totally insufficient, partly due to the slow rate of fire, but also due to the large number of guns that were unserviceable; German pillboxes could be overcome even without adequate artillery but at some cost to the infantry; leaders both senior and subordinate had insufficient time for detailed reconnaissance; the weather conditions slowed every aspect of preparing for the attack; the mud slowed the infantry's response when changing formation; the Reserve Brigade was overtasked, the provision of work parties making it useless as an operational reserve; and the principle used in the battle of 'assault in depth' was justified, but required those units in the rear to be ready to launch the attack without waiting for orders.

A 1917 photograph of two Canadian soldiers standing on top of a captured and comprehensively flooded German pillbox at Passchendaele. Given the exposed position of the soldiers this would have been taken in what was now a rear area, a fact reinforced by the light railway line visible on the right of the photograph (AWM H06971).

There is little that can be criticised in Monash's observations, and his key point, that insufficient time was granted to his division and II ANZAC Corps for the planning and preparation of the attack, should have provided sufficient reason for a postponement. In particular, Monash's comment on the lack of time for senior leaders to complete detailed reconnaissance was germane. According to Australian historian Peter Pedersen in his definitive book on Monash's military career, *Monash as Military Commander*, Monash did not inspect the front line prior to the attack. Given the nature of the ground and Monash's responsibility for designing the division's battle, it can be argued that, despite the obvious time pressures, he should have undertaken such a reconnaissance as a matter of priority. Had he done so, it is possible that Monash would have appreciated the twin follies of sending the 10th Brigade through the swamp of Ravebeek Creek and of making this route the main effort for the attack.

An alternative plan could have seen Monash strengthen the right-hand brigade (9th Brigade) and task it with capturing the village. Under his original plan the 9th Brigade had the advantage of initially advancing along the firmer ground of Passchendaele Ridge, then exploiting to the right as it followed the Ypres—Roulers railway. If

Monash had negotiated brigade and divisional boundaries to allow the 9th Brigade a more direct approach up the ridge to the village, maximum advantage would have been made of the available firm ground. However, instead of using the firmer ground as the focal point of the attack, the reverse occurred. Anxious to maintain contact with the New Zealand Division on his left flank, Monash strengthened the battalion tasked with clearing the village (the 38th Battalion) with an extra company from the 39th Battalion. This extra company would move on the left flank rear of the 38th Battalion to assist in the attack on the village. In case the 10th Brigade became bogged down in village fighting and was unable to link up with the New Zealand Division on the Green Line, the Brigade Reserve (the 39th Battalion less two companies) was also allocated this task—a task that lost its importance once the 10th Brigade limited the extent of its advance to the brigade line E.F. Thus, instead of making maximum use of the firmer ground on the division's right, the divisional attack tasked the left flanking brigade (10th Brigade) with capturing the village. In doing so, the left flanks of the attacking battalions of the 10th Brigade were forced to traverse the swamp-like conditions of Ravebeek Creek between the Bellevue spur and Passchendaele Ridge.

The importance of reconnaissance for the planning process was underscored by the Canadians. Currie conducted a detailed personal reconnaissance prior to the Canadian attack and consequently his plan avoided Ravebeek Creek entirely, recognising that, not only was this area not conducive for the passage of a brigade, but that the difficulty of the ground meant that no physical connection with a flanking division was required. Currie sent his main thrust up the firmer ground of Passchendaele Ridge and it is no accident that it was over this ground that troops made the most progress on both 12 and 26 October.

Passing judgement on a commander's plan with the benefit of hindsight is a problematic exercise. This is particularly true for the First World War in which, because of the high casualty rates, there is a strong temptation for contemporary readers to judge the generals and their staff harshly. But hindsight ignores the reality facing such commanders, the majority of whom were struggling to evolve suitable doctrine and tactics to cope with the newly industrialised battlefield. This learning process was being undertaken in the most unforgiving of conditions—while in contact with the enemy. This judgemental approach is particularly evident when considering the Battle of Passchendaele.

Here the popular view holds that the mud, caused by the almost constant rain since 4 October, made any infantry attack impossible. From this perspective Haig's obstinacy and lack of compassion forced his commanders to undertake an unnecessary attack, despite the impractical conditions. The reality was more nuanced than this. While disquiet over the ground conditions was indeed evident (the British *Official History* records that, until the morning of 11 October, Plumer had assumed that the failure of the Poelcappelle attack was due to the mud rather than the German defences), these concerns are not reflected in the planning. If the ground conditions either side of Passchendaele Ridge represented a major tactical obstacle, the planning and subsequent orders issued by Headquarters II ANZAC Corps and the 3rd Australian Division made no attempt to mitigate the impact of muddy areas on the attack.

Selection of ground aside, Monash had no control over the two factors that did more to decide the outcome of the 3rd Australian Division's battle than any other—the artillery barrage and the New Zealand Division's inability to capture the Bellevue spur. The desultory nature of the Allied barrage on 12 October was a common observation by all participants in the battle. Plumer and Godley's decision to proceed with the attack, despite the acknowledged problems with artillery numbers and supply, doomed the New Zealand attack, which stalled on the German wire in front of the Bellevue spur. What could be accomplished with an adequate artillery preparation was amply demonstrated by Currie although, even then, the capture of the German positions on the Bellevue spur was a tenuous and savage affair.

Artillery planning in 1917 was generally directed and controlled at corps level by the General Officer Commanding Royal Artillery (GOCRA) and the Brigadier General Heavy Artillery (BGHA) in direct response to army-level planning. The GOCRA's duties were to advise the corps commander on artillery matters, but also to coordinate the artillery of the corps and issue orders directly to the heavy artillery groups and the associated commanders of the divisional artillery. The GOCRA effectively had no staff, and coordinated corps artillery assets through a combination of persuasion and good will. That the availability of artillery and munitions would be an issue for the Passchendaele attack was apparent as early as 5 October when the II ANZAC Corps artillery staff noted that, due to the constant movement, munitions supply was not keeping pace with demand. As a result, the II ANZAC GOCRA had already been given permission to reduce the rate of planned artillery fire for the 12 October attack if insufficient munitions were available. The artillery movement and resupply issues were both caused and exacerbated by the strain that rain imposed on the road and track networks within the corps area. This was compounded by the lack of a light rail network. Light railways were by far the most efficient means of moving artillery munitions over sodden ground since, unlike roads, they were largely impervious to wet weather, and easily repaired if broken by shellfire. However, the rapid nature of the BEF advances since the Broodseinde battle meant that II ANZAC Corps had been unable to establish a light rail network to support the artillery in time for the Passchendaele battle. Thus the munitions dumps for the artillery had to be pushed forward by road, with forward emergency dumps still being established on 10 October.

Given the key role that artillery fire played in the 'bite and hold' doctrine, any doubt over the ability to deliver effective artillery fire represented a fundamental weakness in the proposed attack plan for Passchendaele. The artillery commander of the New Zealand Division reported that, owing to the difficulties of crossing the Steenbeek River and the instability of his gun platforms in the mud, effective artillery support for his division could not be guaranteed. Because artillery was generally brigaded as a corps asset, rectifying this weakness was outside the control of both Monash and Major General Russell, the New Zealand divisional commander. Plumer and Godley were aware of these deficiencies and ordered that, if a battery was short of guns due to the mud, it should increase its rate of fire to compensate for this deficiency. However this ignored the other half of the problem, which was the difficulty of keeping the remaining artillery supplied with sufficient shells to maintain this increased rate of fire. The shortcomings in artillery support represented a significant planning deficiency, caused by the speed of the advances since 4 October, the poor ground conditions for the movement of artillery and munitions and the desire of Haig and Plumer to capitalise on what they perceived as a weakness in the German defence. This shortcoming in artillery support had significant consequences for the conduct of the battle.

The performance of the Australian soldiers on 12 October was all that could be expected of experienced troops who had fought a major battle at Broodseinde a mere eight days earlier. Residual tension and fatigue from Broodseinde would have been compounded by the difficult approach march to the start line of the

Passchendaele attack, the casualties from German shelling and the discomfort of lying in the cold and rain prior to the actual attack. Like most troops suffering fatigue, this would have been swept aside in the initial excitement of 'going over the top', but once the attack stalled, the slump in morale would have been all the more dramatic given the privations already endured.

The shattering impact of the German machine-gun fire on the left flank of the 10th Brigade halted its attack almost before it started and the men struggled to consolidate on the Red Line. Their despair after the battle was palpable. The 37th Battalion history lamented: 'The previous attack [Broodseinde] had left the battalion in good spirits. This one left it in the depths of depression.' The 39th Battalion told a similar story:

> The experiences which befell the 39th on the swampy flats beyond Ypres were the worst and the most trying of the whole war. Throughout this awful nightmare—this Battle of Passchendaele may justly be so described—the men had lived up to the highest traditions of their country, and had borne the dreadful ordeal with patience and gallantry.

While the 10th Brigade managed to conduct a controlled withdrawal under the command of

Major Giblin, the same was not true for the 9th Brigade. There is little doubt that its withdrawal from the Blue Line was not conducted in a controlled manner. Bean describes the 9th Brigade withdrawal in vivid terms: '...the retiring troops, being without orders as to the position to be taken up, streaming back past Milne's headquarters.'

The 9th Brigade Court of Inquiry had an implied task of determining whether the withdrawal was caused by panic. The testimony given during the inquiry provides some insight into the state of the 9th Brigade soldiers at the height of the battle. Major Carr described the possible 'trigger' for the withdrawal:

> I saw that the men on the left flank had already started to move back. The bombardment at this time was particularly heavy on the left flank and this doubtless caused the men to act on my warning instead of the actual order to move back. I then decided to fall back along the Red Line and gave orders accordingly.

Faced with an untenable situation on a forward slope and under direct fire from German batteries, the troops took matters into their own hands. Sergeant George Burgess, at the time of the battle a lance corporal in D Company, 35th Battalion, was asked:

Question of Court: Who gave the order to evacuate to the Red Line?

Answer: I don't know.

Question of the Court: Did you receive a warning to prepare to withdraw to the Red Line?

Answer: No.

Private George Bain, also of the 35th Battalion, provided the court a statement in which he said: '...word was passed to us from a shell hole to our right to evacuate the Red Line. We did so...'

Word of mouth and second-hand information became sufficient to initiate a mass withdrawal from the Blue Line, which only halted once the troops had gained the relative safety of the 11th Brigade lines. The example of the 9th Brigade shows that, on any one day, even battle-hardened troops will have their limits. When placed in an exposed tactical position, suffering heavy causalities and in the absence of strong leadership, soldiers will make their own decisions. Major Carr's warning order to prepare to withdraw triggered a response that the soldiers already entertained. Only resolute direction and support for Major Carr from 9th Brigade Headquarters would have halted this withdrawal—support that he did not receive.

Writing home on 18 October 1917, Monash said of the 3rd Australian Division: 'Our men are being put into the hottest fighting and are being sacrificed in hare-brained ventures like Bullecourt and Passchendaele.' Monash's sentiment spoke of the tragedy suffered by both the Australian and New Zealand divisions on 12 October 1917, which saw proficient and experienced troops thrown at strong defences without adequate preparation. While this was surely true, neither Godley nor Monash could absolve himself of responsibility for a plan which took little account of the state of the ground around Passchendaele. The outcome of this inadequate planning and preparation was heavy losses for the two divisions, their soldiers wasted and morale damaged without the consolation of even local gains. It was surely a small comfort to the soldiers of the 3rd Australian Division and the New Zealand Division that it was left to Currie and the Canadian Corps to show that Passchendaele could be seized, despite the conditions.

A section of the Tyne Cot Cemetery which contains 11,848 graves including 609 Australians, one of four memorials to those killed during the Third Ypres campaign. The date of this photograph is unknown, but it was clearly taken before the design of the current consolidated cemetery in 1927 (AWM H12653).

A view of Tyne Cot Cemetery in 2018 (image courtesy of Bill Frost).

BIBLIOGRAPHY

OFFICIAL HISTORIES

Bean, C.E.W, *Official History of Australia in the War of 1914-18*, Vol. IV, The AIF in France 1917, Angus & Robertson, Sydney, 1940.

Edmonds, J.E., *History of the Great War, Military Operations France and Belgium 1916, Sir Douglas Haig's Command to the 1st July, Battle of the Somme*, MacMillan and Co., London, 1932.

_____, *History of the Great War, Military Operations France and Belgium 1917*, Vol. II, 7th June-10th November, Messines and Third Ypres (Passchendaele), His Majesty's Stationery Office, London, 1948.

Miles, W., *History of the Great War, Military Operations France and Belgium 1916*, 2nd July 1916 to the end of the Battles of the Somme, MacMillan and Co., London, 1938.

Nicholson, G.W.L., *Official History of the Canadian Army in the First World War. Canadian Expeditionary Force 1914-1919*, Queen's Printer and Controller of Stationary, Ottawa, 1962.

Stewart, H., *Official History of New Zealand's Effort in the Great War*, Vol. II, *France. The New Zealand Division 1916-1919*, Whitcombe and Tombs Limited, Wellington, 1921.

BOOKS AND BOOK CHAPTERS

Allen, P.V. & Committee (eds), *The Thirty-Ninth. The History of the Thirty-Ninth Battalion, AIF*, G.W. Green and Sons Pty Ltd, Melbourne, 1934.

Bailey, J., 'British Artillery in the Great War' in *British Fighting Methods in the Great War*, P. Griffith (ed), Frank Cass Publishers, London, 1998.

Beach, J., *Haig's Intelligence. GHQ and the German Army, 1916-1918*, Cambridge University Press, Cambridge, 2015.

Beckett, I., Bowman, T., and Connelly, M., *The British Army and the First World War*, Cambridge University Press, Cambridge, 2017.

Brown, I.M., *British Logistics on the Western Front*, Praeger Publishers, Westport, Connecticut, 1998.

Cave, N., *Passchendaele. The Fight for the Village*, Pen and Sword, South Yorkshire, 2013.

Clark, M.A., *Carmichael's 1000 Their Triumphs and Their Trials. A History of the 36th Battalion AIF*, Galloping Press, Kirrawee, NSW, 2014.

Cuttriss, G.P., *'Over the Top' with the Third Australian Division*, Charles H. Kelly, London, 1918.

Dennis, P., Grey, J., Morris, E. and Prior, R. (eds), *The Oxford Companion to Australian Military History*, Oxford University Press (2nd edn), Melbourne, Victoria, 2008.

Fairey, E., *The 38th Battalion AIF. The Story and Official History of the 38th Battalion AIF*, Bendigo Advertiser Pty Ltd and Cambridge Press, Bendigo, Victoria, 1920.

Godley, A., *Life of an Irish Soldier*, Butler and Tanner Ltd., London, 1939.

Gough, H., *The Fifth Army*, Hodder and Stoughton, London, 1931.

Green, F.C., *The Fortieth, A Record of the 40th Battalion, A.I.F,* printed for the 40th Battalion Association, Government Printer, 1922.

Griffith, P., *Battle Tactics of the Western Front,* Yale University Press, New Haven and London, 1994.

_____, *Fortifications of the Western Front,* Osprey Publishing, Oxford, 2004.

Harington, C., *Plumer of Messines,* Butler and Tanner Ltd, London, 1935.

Holloway, D.C., *Combat Colonels of the AIF in the Great War,* Big Sky Publishing Pty Ltd, Newport, NSW, 2014.

Horner, D., *The Gunners. A History of Australian Artillery,* Allen and Unwin, St Leonards, 1995.

Humphries, M.O., *The Selected Papers of Sir Arthur Currie, Diaries, Letters, and Report to the Ministry, 1917-1933,* Press of Wilfrid Laurier University, Waterloo, Ontario, 2008.

Lloyd George, D., *War Memoirs of David Lloyd George,* Vol. III, Ivor Nicholson and Watson, London, 1934.

MacDougall, A.K., *John Monash, War Letters of General Monash*, Black Inc, Melbourne, 2015.

McGibbon, I., *The Oxford Companion to New Zealand Military History*, Oxford University Press, Auckland, 2000.

McNicol, N.G., *The Thirty-Seventh. "History of the Thirty-Seventh Battalion A.I.F"*, Modern Printing Co. Pty. Ltd., Melbourne, 1936.

Palazzo, A., *Defenders of Australia: The 3rd Australian Division, 1916-1991*, Australian Military History Publications, Loftus, NSW, 2002.

Patten, G. 'Indirect Fire. The AIF's Artillery and Mortars on the Western Front' in *The AIF in Battle. How the Australian Imperial Force Fought, 1914-1918*, J. Bou (ed), Melbourne University Press, Melbourne, 2016.

Pedersen, P.A., *Monash as Military Commander*, Melbourne University Press, Melbourne, 1992.

Prentiss, A.M., *Chemicals in War*, McGraw-Hill, New York and London, 1937.

Prior, R. and Wilson, T., *Passchendaele the Untold Story*, Yale University Press, New Haven and London, 1996.

Sheffield, G. and Bourne, J., *Douglas Haig. War Diaries and Letters 1914-1918*, Weidenfeld and Nicolson, London, 2005.

Sheldon, J., *The German Army at Passchendaele*, Pen and Sword, South Yorkshire, 2014.

Smith., A.H., *Do Unto Others. Counter Bombardment in Australia's Military Campaigns*, Big Sky Publishing, Newport, NSW, 2011.

Steele, H., *The Canadians in France 1915-1918*, T. Fisher Unwin Ltd, London, 1920.

Steel, N. and Hart, P. *Passchendaele. The Sacrificial Ground*, Cassell, London, 2007.

Stevenson, R., *The War with Germany*, Oxford University Press, South Melbourne, Victoria, 2015.

Stone, D., *The Kaiser's Army, The German Army in World War One*, Conway, Bloomsbury Publishing, New York, 2015.

GOVERNMENT PUBLICATIONS/ARCHIVES

AWM Unit Records Collected by Henry Arthur Goddard, Sub-series 3: 9th Infantry Brigade (1916-1918), Item 3DRL/2379.

AWM4, AIF Unit War Diaries 1914-18 War, General Staff, Headquarters 2nd ANZAC Corps, October 1917, Item 1/32/20 Part 2. II ANZAC Corps Order No 90, dated 8 October 1917.

AWM4, AIF Unit War Diaries 1914-18 War, General Staff, Headquarters 2nd ANZAC Corps, October 1917, Item 1/32/20 Part 2. II ANZAC Instructions for the Offensive, Instruction Number 2, dated 1 October 1917.

AWM4, AIF Unit War Diaries 1914-18 War, General Staff, Headquarters 2nd ANZAC Corps, October 1917, Item 1/32/20 Part 2. II ANZAC Instructions for the Offensive, Instruction Number 3, Contact Patrols, dated 1 October 1917.

AWM4, AIF Unit War Diaries 1914-18 War, General Staff, Headquarters 2nd ANZAC Corps, October 1917, Item 1/32/20 Part 2. II ANZAC

Instructions for the Offensive, Instruction Number 4, dated 1 October 1917.

AWM4, AIF Unit War Diaries 1914-18 War, General Staff, Headquarters 2nd ANZAC Corps, October 1917, Item 1/32/20 Part 2. II ANZAC Corps Instruction No.8 (Provisional), dated 8 October 1917.

AWM4, AIF Unit War Diaries 1914-18 War, General Staff, Headquarters 2nd ANZAC Corps, October 1917, Item 1/32/20 Part 2. II ANZAC Corps Instruction No.8, dated 10 October 1917.

AWM4, AIF Unit War Diaries 1914-18 War, General Staff, Headquarters 2nd ANZAC Corps, October 1917, Item 1/32/20 Part 3, 2nd ANZAC Artillery Instructions, Appendix 7, dated 5 October 1917.

AWM4, AIF Unit War Diaries 1914-18 War, General Staff, Headquarters 3rd Australian Division, October 1917, Item 1/46/12 Part 7.

AWM4, AIF Unit War Diaries 1914-18 War, General Staff, Headquarters 3rd Australian Division, October 1917, Item 1/46/12 Part 4. "Y.B.G.S.C." No.26 dated 9 October, "Y.B.G.S.C." No.27 and "Y.B.G.S.C." No.28 dated

10 October and "Y.B.G.S.C." No.29 and "Y.B.G.S.C." No.30 dated 11 October 1917.

AWM4, AIF Unit War Diaries 1914-18 War, General Staff, Headquarters 3rd Australian Division, October 1917, Item 1/46/12 Part 7. Third Australian Division, Reference No. G. 123/2/6 dated 1 November 1917.

AWM4, AIF Unit War Diaries 1914-18 War, Administrative Staff, Headquarters 3rd Australian Division, October 1917, Item 1/47/, Administrative War Diary, dated 11 October 1917.

AWM4 AIF Unit War Diaries 1914-18 War, Assistant Director of Medical Services, 3rd Australian Division, October 1917, Item 26/20/13.

AWM4, AIF Unit War Diaries, 1914-18 War, 12th Infantry Brigade War Diary, Item Number 23/12/20, October 1917. Report on Operations by 12th Australian Infantry Brigade Near Zonnebeke, 11th—14th October 1917.

AWM4, AIF Unit War Diaries, 1914-18 War, 10th Infantry Brigade, Item Number 23/10/12, October 1917. Tenth Australian Infantry Brigade Order No.68 dated 9 October 1917.

AWM4, AIF Unit War Diaries, 1914-18 War, 10th Infantry Brigade, Item Number 23/10/12, October 1917. 10th Australian Infantry Brigade Order No.68, Appendix 'F' dated 10 October 1917.

AWM4, AIF Unit War Diaries, 1914-18 War, 10th Infantry Brigade War Diary, Item Number 23/10/12, October 1917.

AWM4, AIF Unit War Diaries, 1914-18 War, 9th Infantry Brigade War Diary, Item Number 23/10/12, October 1917. Report of the Operations Carried Out On 12-10-17.

AWM4, AIF Unit War Diaries 1914-18 War, 40th Infantry Battalion, October 1917 Appendices, Item 23/57/19 Part 1.

AWM4, AIF Unit War Diaries 1914-18 War, 38th Infantry Battalion, October 1917, Item 23/55/17.

AWM4, AIF Unit War Diaries 1914-18 War, 37th Infantry Battalion, October 1917, Item 23/54/15. Ypres – Phase 5, Part Played by the 37th Battalion, Friday 12th October 1917, dated 1 November 1917.

AWM4, AIF Unit War Diaries 1914-18 War, 36th Infantry Battalion, October 1917, Item 23/53/12.

AWM4, AIF Unit War Diaries 1914-18 War, 35th Infantry Battalion, October 1917, Item 23/52/4.

AWM4, AIF Unit War Diaries 1914-18 War, 34th Infantry Battalion, October 1917, Item 23/51/12.

AWM4, AIF Unit War Diaries 1914-18 War, 33th Infantry Battalion, October 1917, Item 23/50/12.

AWM4 AIF Unit War Diaries 1914-18 War, 9th Australian Field Ambulance, October 1917, Item 25/52/7.

AWM4 AIF Unit War Diaries 1914-18 War, 3rd Australian Division Salvage Company, October 1917, Item 19/5/9.

AWM, Monash First World War Papers, Personal Files Box 16, 7 September – 9 October 1917, Third Australian Division correspondence to Headquarters II ANZAC Corps, dated 9 October 1917.

AWM, Monash First World War Papers, Personal Files Box 16, 7 September – 9 October 1917, Third Australian Division correspondence to Headquarters II ANZAC Corps, dated 10 October 1917.

AWM, Monash First World War Papers, Personal Files Box 16, 7 September – 9 October 1917, Headquarters Second Army correspondence from Major General Harington to Major General Monash, dated 11 October 1917.

AWM, Monash First World War Papers, Personal Files Box 16, 7 September – 9 October 1917, Major General Monash note (42) to 9th and 10th Brigades, dated 12 October 1917.

AWM, Monash First World War Papers, Personal Files Box 16, 9 October – 31 October 1917, Message to 2 ANZAC, dated 12 October 1917.

AWM, Monash First World War Papers, Personal Files Box 16, 7 September – 9 October 1917, Major General Monash note (45) to 2nd ANZAC, dated 13 October 1917.

AWM, Monash First World War Papers, Personal Files Box 16, 7 September – 9 October 1917,

Major General Monash note (46) to Brigade, dated 13 October 1917.

AWM, Monash First World War Papers, Personal Files Box 16, 7 September – 9 October 1917, Special Order to Third Australian Division, released by Q.M.G Third Australian Division, dated 13 October 1917.

AWM, Monash First World War Papers, Personal Files Box 16, 7 September – 9 October 1917, Message and Signal From Lieutenant General Godley to Major General Monash dated 13 October 1917.

AWM, Monash First World War Papers, Personal Files Box 16, 7 September – 9 October 1917, Lieutenant General Godley to Second Army, dated 13 October 1917.

AWM, Monash First World War Papers, Personal Files Box 16, 7 September – 9 October 1917, Third Infantry Division, correspondence from Major General Monash to Headquarters 2nd ANZAC Corps dated 14 October 1917.

AWM, Monash First World War Papers, Personal Files Box 16, 7 September – 9 October 1917,

9th Infantry Brigade casualty report to GOC Third Australian, dated 30 October 1917.

General Staff (Intelligence), General Headquarters, Summary of Recent Information Regarding the German Army and its Methods, Pamphlet S.S. 537, 1917.

General Staff (Intelligence), General Headquarters, Translation of The Principles of Command in the Defensive Battle in Position Warfare, Pamphlet S.S. 249, 1 September 1917.

General Staff (Intelligence), Advanced General Headquarters, Translation of a German Document, New Defensive Tactics, S.S. 710, 14 November 1917.

General Staff, Intelligence Section, American Expeditionary Forces, Histories of Two Hundred and Fifty-One Divisions of the German Army Which Participated in the War (1914-1918), 1919.

General Staff (Intelligence), General Headquarters, Captured German Document. Notes on the Construction of Positions on the Ypres Battle Front for the Coming Winter, S.S. 701, 2 October 1917.

General Staff Translation, Prussian War Ministry, Manual of Position Warfare for Al, Arms, Part 1. The Construction of Field Positions. (Stellungsbau), Berlin 1916, Darling and Son, Ltd, London, May 1917.

General Staff, The Tactical Summary of Machine Gun Operations, No.2 Pamphlet S.S. 201, November-December 1917.

Land Service, Handbook of the Stokes 3-inch Trench Mortar Equipments, His Majesty's Stationery office, 1920.

Report upon the Department of Defence for the period 1/7/1914 to 30/6/1917, Australian National Archives, Series Number M394.

The War Office, Notes for Infantry Officers on Trench Warfare, His Majesty's Stationery Office, London, 1916.

CONFERENCE PAPERS

Cook, T., 'Storm Troops: Combat Effectiveness and the Canadian Corps in 1917' in *1917 Tactics, Training and Technology*, Proceedings of The Chief of Army's Military History Conference 2007, P.

Dennis and J. Grey (eds), Australian Military History Publications, Loftus, NSW, 2007.

Doughty, R.A., 'How did France Weather the Troubles of 1917?' in *1917 Tactics, Training and Technology*, Proceedings of The Chief of Army's Military History Conference 2007, P. Dennis and J. Grey (eds), Australian Military History Publications, Loftus, NSW, 2007.

Foley, R.T., 'The Other Side of the Wire: The German Army in 1917' in *1917 Tactics, Training and Technology*, Proceedings of The Chief of Army's Military History Conference 2007, P. Dennis and J. Grey (eds), Australian Military History Publications, Loftus, NSW, 2007.

Sheffield, G., 'Haig and the British Expeditionary Force in 1917' in *1917 Tactics, Training and Technology*, Proceedings of The Chief of Army's Military History Conference 2007, P. Dennis and J. Grey (eds), Australian Military History Publications, Loftus, NSW, 2007.

Stephenson, R., 'The 1st Australian Division in 1917: A Snapshot' in *1917 Tactics, Training and Technology*, Proceedings of The Chief of Army's Military History Conference 2007, P. Dennis and

J. Grey (eds), Australian Military History Publications, Loftus, NSW, 2007.

JOURNAL ARTICLES

Foley, R.T., 'Learning War's Lessons: The German Army and the Battle of the Somme 1916', *Journal of Military History*, April 2011, Vol 75, Issue 2.

Lee, R., 'Planning the World War One Battle: A Complex Process', unpublished Australian Army History Unit paper, 2016.

Zecevic, M., 'The Influence of geology on the course and outcome of the Third Battle of Ypres', *The Mining-Geology-Petroleum Engineering Bulletin*, Issue 10.1177/rgn.2016.1.1.

WEBSITES

The Australian Dictionary of Biography at: http://adb.anu.edu.au/biography

The Australian War Memorial at: http://www.awm.gov.au

BACK COVER MATERIAL

THE BATTLE OF PASSCHENDAELE

The Battle for Passchendaele or 12 October 1917 was one of the epic struggles of the First World War. British Field Marshal Douglas Haig allocated II ANZAC Corps to capture Passchendaele village, with Major General Monash's 3rd Australian Division and the New Zealand Division leading the attack. For both divisions the battle was a bloody debacle. Monash's division starred the battle with 5800 men and, just 24 hours later, could only muster 2600, suffering horrendous losses for a small territorial gain which was later relinquished. The New Zealand Division was trapped in front of the German wire and barely moved from its start line, suffering one of its highest casualty rates of the war. Fought in conditions which seemed to preclude any chance of success, the battle has become a metaphor for pointless sacrifice.

After the battle the British and Australian leadership were unanimous in placing blame for the defeat on the all-pervasive mud. Monash, writing to his wife, believed that his plan 'would have succeeded in normal conditions'. Yet, two weeks later, in similar weather and terrain,

Lieutenant General Curries Canadian Corps succeeded where Monash and Godley's II ANZAG Corps did not. The central focus of this book is a detailed analysis of the 3rd Australian Division's plan and execution of the attack on Passchendaele, By examining the differences between the Australian and Canadian plans for the capture Passchendaele, the author casts this iconic battle in a completely different light. It is a re-examination that is long overdue.

Index

A
Admiralty, *9, 21, 282*
Allied forces, *13, 16, 26, 30*
attacks between June and November 1917,
  'bite and hold' tactics, *100, 101*
  Flanders offensive, *9*
  intelligence, *115*
  strategy and tactics, *58, 62, 65, 68, 71, 73, 78*
Arras, *9, 13, 16, 24, 286*
artillery, *9, 16, 71*
artillery barrage, *101, 176, 178, 189, 201, 204, 211, 260*
artillery fire, *48, 104*
4.5-inch howitzers, *91, 131, 133, 134, 189*
Allied, *48, 100, 101, 104, 115, 260*
Australian, *51, 131, 133, 134, 145, 150, 249*
  barrage, *24, 44, 51, 57, 65, 68, 87, 101, 128, 131, 134, 145, 152, 161, 176, 178, 189, 201, 204, 211, 226, 245, 249, 260, 268, 276*
  box barrage, *24*
BL 60-pounders, *131, 133, 134, 189, 194, 249*
  gas, *87*
  lifting, *65*
  standing, *65*
British, *21, 24, 34, 37, 40, 44, 48, 51, 65, 68, 286*
Canadian Corps, *249*
creeping barrage, *24, 65, 68*
counter-battery plan, *37*
divisional, *68*
doctrine of total destruction, *65*
field gun, *21, 68, 91, 100, 134, 189*
fire plan, *24*
Forward Observation Officer (FOO), *68*
German, *24, 37, 40, 58, 65, 91, 100, 101, 104, 113,*

115, 169, 174, 178, 180, 185, 204, 207, 217, 218, 245, 257, 260, 276, 284
howitzers, *21, 68, 91, 100, 131, 133, 134, 189*
Ordnance QF 4.5-inch, *131, 133, 134, 189*
M1916 77mm field gun, *91, 100*
M1916 105mm light field howitzer, *91, 100*
mortars, *68, 91, 100, 101, 113, 133, 134, 143, 152, 161, 204*
mud and, *209*
Ordnance QF 4.5-inch howitzers, *131, 133, 134, 189*
Ordnance QF 18-pounders, *131, 133, 134, 189, 194, 249*
reserve, *68*
Stokes 3.2-inch (81.2mm) trench mortar, *143, 161, 204*
trench mortars, *100, 101, 113, 133, 143, 152, 161*
tactical thinking, *65*

Augustus Wood, *189, 218*
Australian Imperial Force (AIF),
  I ANZAC Corps, *21, 44, 51, 57, 124, 145, 260*
  II ANZAC Corps, *21, 24, 30, 48, 51, 57, 84, 123, 124, 128, 131, 133, 134, 145, 174, 176, 178, 184, 185, 188, 209, 211, 232, 242, 249, 255, 260*
  1st Division, *78*
  2nd Division, *78*
  3rd Division, *78, 84, 87, 89, 123, 124, 128, 131, 133, 134, 141, 143, 145, 148, 150, 152, 154, 156, 157, 161, 162, 167, 169, 172, 174, 176, 178, 180, 183, 184, 185, 188, 189, 194, 195, 197, 201, 204, 207, 209, 211, 214, 217, 218, 221, 223, 226, 228, 229, 232, 235, 238, 240, 242, 245*
  approach march, *167, 169, 172, 174, 176*
  assessment of 3rd Australian Division's plan and performance,
    barrage, *176, 178*

casualties, *51, 87, 169, 174, 184, 185, 189, 201, 204, 209, 211, 217, 240, 242, 257*
expansion and reorganisation, *78*
holding front line, *235, 238, 240, 242, 245*
raising and training, *78, 81, 84, 87, 89*
Reserve Brigade, *245*
Supporting Brigade, *245*
4th Brigade, *78, 81, 226*
6th Battalion, *156*
7th Battalion, *156*
8th Brigade, *78*
9th Brigade, *78, 134, 141, 148, 150, 152, 161, 169, 174, 176, 184, 188, 189, 201, 204, 207, 211, 214, 217, 218, 223, 226, 235, 240, 245, 257, 260, 265*
10th Brigade, *78, 134, 141, 148, 152, 154, 156, 161, 162, 167, 169, 172, 178, 180, 184, 185, 188, 189, 201, 204, 207, 211, 214, 217, 218, 226, 228, 235, 240, 242, 245, 257, 265*
11th Brigade, *78, 141, 148, 161, 162, 204, 211, 214, 226, 235, 242, 245*
148th Brigade, *242, 245*
15th Battalion, *162*
33rd Battalion, *78, 87, 152, 174, 204, 211, 214, 217, 218, 240*
34th Battalion, *87, 152, 174, 189, 195, 201, 211, 217, 226, 240*
35th Battalion, *152, 174, 201, 217, 218, 226, 240*
36th Battalion, *78, 152, 174, 201, 217, 218, 240*
37th Battalion, *78, 141, 154, 161, 167, 169, 176, 178, 180, 185, 189, 240*
39th Battalion, *78, 87, 113, 134, 154, 161, 169, 176, 188, 211, 214, 217, 240, 242*
40th Battalion, *78, 154, 169, 180, 183, 185, 188, 211, 214, 232, 242*
41st Battalion, *78, 214*
42nd Battalion, *78*
43rd Battalion, *78, 214*
44th Battalion, *78*

Australian Official History of Australia in the War 1914-1918, *54, 154*
   barbed wire, *62*

B

battles,
   Arras, *9, 13, 16, 24, 286*
Broodseinde, *34, 40, 44, 48, 51, 54, 58, 81, 87, 89, 104, 113, 124, 145, 148, 176, 184, 188, 194, 257, 284, 286*
   Langemarck, *34, 37, 40, 41, 44*
   Menin Road, *2, 44, 48, 58, 123, 167, 242*
   Messines, *9, 16, 19, 21, 24, 26, 30, 34, 41, 44, 81, 84, 87, 89, 113, 183, 184, 188, 195, 278, 282, 284*
   Pilckem Ridge, *9, 16, 30, 34, 167*
   Poelcappelle, *48, 54, 57, 58, 87, 115, 123, 124, 148, 154, 169, 217, 286*
   Polygon Wood, *40, 44, 48, 58*
   Verdun, *9, 13, 58, 89, 282*
   Ypres, First Battle of, *6, 9*
Beach, J., *286*
Bean, C.E.W, *54, 84, 154, 176*
Bellevue spur, *113, 184, 185, 188, 189, 201, 204, 207, 209, 211, 214, 245, 257, 260, 265*
Birdwood, Lieutenant General Sir William, *51, 81, 128, 145*
Blue Line, *124, 134, 152, 154, 180, 184, 201, 204, 207, 211, 217, 218, 223, 226, 238*
British Expeditionary Force (BEF),
   First Army, *6, 24*
   Second Army, *9, 21, 24, 30, 34, 40, 44, 48, 51, 57, 58, 87, 123, 145, 245, 249, 286*
   Fourth Army, *9*
   Fifth Army, *21, 27, 30, 34, 37, 40, 41, 44, 48, 51, 167, 249, 260*
   49th British Division, *148*
   66th British Division, *148*
   casualties, *40, 58*

intelligence, *286*
Small Box Respirator, *242*
British Official History of the Great War, *34, 57, 278, 286*
Broodseinde, *34, 40, 44, 48, 51, 54, 58, 81, 87, 89, 104, 113, 124, 145, 148, 176, 184, 188, 194, 257, 284, 286*

C

Cabinet Committee on War Policy, *282*
Campagne les Boulonnais, *245*
Canadian Corps, *123, 232, 242, 249, 252, 254, 255, 257, 260, 265, 268, 270, 273*
    1st Canadian Division, *268, 270*
    2nd Canadian Division, *268*
    3rd Canadian Division, *260, 265*
    4th Canadian Division, *260, 265*
    2nd Brigade, *270*
    3rd Battalion, *268*
    6th Brigade, *268*
    8th Brigade, *265*
    10th Brigade, *257, 260, 270*
    12th Brigade, *265*
    43rd Battalion, *260*
    52nd Battalion, *260*
    artillery, *249, 260*
    attacks on Passchendaele, *249, 255, 257, 260, 265, 268, 270, 273*
    casualties, *257, 260, 273*
    Victoria Crosses, *265*
Canadian Official History of the Canadian Army in the First World War, *249*
Cannan, Brigadier General James, *148, 162*
Carr, Major Henry, *218, 221, 223, 226*
casualties, *257, 260, 273*
    Allied, *278*
    Australian, *51, 87, 169, 174, 184, 185, 189, 201, 204, 209, 211, 217, 240, 242, 257*
    British Army, *40, 58*
    Canadian Corps, *123, 232, 242, 249, 252, 254, 255, 257, 260, 265, 268, 270, 273*

Charteris, Brigadier General John, *286*
Cloth Hall, Ypres, *254*
conferences, *9, 13, 16, 21, 30, 34, 40, 48, 57, 134, 214, 249*
Crest Farm, *185, 188, 201, 209, 214, 265, 270*
Curragh Mutiny, *27*
Currie, Lieutenant General Sir Arthur, *232, 249, 252, 254, 255, 257, 260, 268, 282*
Cuttriss, Padre George, *78, 178*

D
Dab Trench, *169*
defence in depth, *100, 101, 113, 226*
Dixon, Captain William, *218*

E
Edmonds, J.E., *286*
Enlist Farm, *217, 218*
    field ambulances, *228, 229, 232*
    firepower, *44, 54, 58, 65, 68, 71, 73, 100, 101, 104, 161, 180*

F
First World War, *276*
Forward Zone, *101, 104, 145*
French Army, *9, 13, 16, 54, 58, 78, 282*
First Army, *30, 34, 37, 40*
French, Field Marshal Sir John, *6*
Fry, Major Walter, *226*
'F' Track, *174*

G
German, *278, 286*
Gadd, Captain Richard, *218*
Gallipoli campaign, *78, 81, 128, 150, 156, 162, 189*
gas,
    attacks, *242, 245*
    masks, *169, 174*
    mustard, *242*
    shells, *169, 174, 242*
    sneezing, *242*
    tear, *242*
Geelong High School, *156*
Gellibrand, Brigadier General, *156*

German 7.6cm (light) minenwerfer, *143*
German Army, *13, 40, 51, 54, 57, 65, 89, 91, 100, 101, 104, 108, 109, 113, 115, 116, 122, 180, 249, 265, 276, 282, 284, 286*
   Army Group Rupprecht, *54, 286*
   1st Bavarian Reserve Corps, *286*
   3rd Reserve Infantry Division, *115*
   20th Infantry Division, *115*
   195th Infantry Division, *104, 113, 115, 145*
   101st Reserve Infantry Brigade, *104*
   5th Jager Regiment, *115*
   6th Jager Regiment, *104*
   8th Jager Regiment, *104, 115*
   200th Field Artillery Regiment, *104*
   233rd Reserve Infantry Regiment, *104, 115*
   artillery, *91, 100*
   casualties, *278, 286*
   defensive doctrine, *100, 101, 104*
   divisions, *89*
   gas attacks, *242, 245*
   Instruction for Position Warfare for All Arms, *100*
   organisation of German infantry division, *104*
   pattern machine-guns, *104, 108*
   strategic status on the Western Front, *89, 91, 100*
   The Construction of Field Positions (Stellungsbau), *116*
   The Principles of Command in the Defensive Battle in Position Warfare, *101*
   U-boat operations, *21, 89, 282*

German gas barrage, *87, 100*
Gheluvelt Plateau, *9, 16, 30, 34, 37, 40, 44, 48*
Giblin, Major Lyndhurst, *183, 184, 185, 214, 218*
Godley, Lieutenant General Sir Alexander, *51, 124, 128, 134, 189, 211, 214, 235, 238, 240*
Gough, General Sir Charles, *27*
Gough, Lieutenant General Sir Hubert, *9, 13, 21, 27, 30, 34, 37, 40, 41, 44, 48, 54, 57, 65, 167, 249, 284*
Great Depression, *254*
Green Line, *124, 128, 134, 145, 152, 154, 161, 201, 204, 211, 249, 255, 268*

H

Haig, Field Marshal Sir Douglas, *4, 6, 9, 13, 16, 19, 21, 24, 27, 30, 34, 37, 40, 44, 48, 51, 54, 57, 65, 78, 87, 123, 180, 194, 249, 260, 273, 276*
   attrition strategy, *9, 16, 276, 284, 286*
   operational objectives, devolution of, *282, 284, 286*
Haig's Intelligence. GHQ and the German Army 1916-1918 (Beach), *286*
Harington, Major General Charles, *145, 286*
Heine House, *189*
Henderson, Lieutenant Colonel Robert, *188*

J

Jefferies, Captain Clarence, *189, 195, 197, 201*
Jellicoe, Admiral John, *21*
Joffre, Marshal Joseph, *9*

K

Kiggell, Lieutenant General Sir Launcelot, *249*
'K' Track, *167, 169, 172*

L

Langemarck, *34, 37, 40, 41, 44*
Lloyd George, D., *13, 16, 21*

Ludendorff, General Erich, *100, 101, 104*
Lewis machine-guns, *71, 73, 240*
   Vickers medium machine-guns, *71, 73, 134, 152, 161, 204, 226, 245*
   S.S. 201, The Tactical Summary of Machine Gun Operations, *73*

M

machine-guns, *24, 44, 58, 65, 68, 84, 113, 115, 116, 122, 178, 180, 184, 189, 201, 209, 217, 238*
Macmullen, Lieutenant Colonel, *9*
Main Line of Resistance, *101, 104*
Martin, Lieutenant Colonel Ernst, *240*
McDowell, Major J., *226*
McNicoll, Brigadier General Walter, *148, 156, 157, 188*
McNicol, Lieutenant Norman, *176*

Menin Road, *2, 44, 48, 58, 123, 167, 242*
Messines, *9, 16, 19, 21, 24, 26, 30, 34, 41, 44, 81, 84, 87, 89, 113, 183, 184, 188, 195, 278, 282, 284*
Meetcheele, *113, 188, 265, 268*
Mills bombs, *71, 228*
Milne, Lieutenant Colonel John, *201, 204, 217, 218, 226, 238, 240*
Monash, Major General John, *78, 81, 84, 87, 115, 134, 145, 148, 156, 161, 162, 174, 176, 178, 180, 185, 209, 211, 214, 226, 232, 235, 238, 240, 242, 245, 257, 260, 282*
Morrison, Brigadier Edward, *249, 257*
Morshead, Lieutenant Colonel Leslie, *223, 240*
mortars, *68, 91, 134, 152*
   Stokes, *143, 161, 204*
   1919 Handbook of the M.L. Stokes 3-inch trench Mortar Equipments, *143*

trench, *100, 101, 113, 133, 143, 152, 161*
mud, influence of, *286*

N

New Zealand Division, *21, 48, 57, 123, 124, 128, 134, 141, 184, 188, 189, 204, 207, 209, 211, 214, 226, 232, 238, 240, 260*
Nivelle, Marshal Robert, *9, 13, 282*

O

Ordnance QF 4.5-inch howitzers, *131, 133, 134, 189*
Ordnance QF 18-pounders, *131, 133, 134, 189, 194, 249*

P

Pas-de-Calais area, *245*
Passchendaele Ridge, *30, 44, 48, 57, 113, 124, 188, 257, 260, 270, 273, 276*
Petain, General Philippe, *13, 16, 19, 40*
pillboxes, *24, 113, 115, 116, 184, 185, 188, 189, 228, 260, 265*

Pilckem Ridge, *9, 16, 30, 34, 167*
planning II ANZAC Corps, *124, 134*
3rd Australian Division, *134, 141, 143, 145, 148*
9th Brigade, *152*
10th Brigade, *152, 154, 161*
11th Brigade, *161*
Plumer, Lieutenant General Sir Hubert, *9, 21, 30, 34, 40, 44, 48, 51, 54, 57, 123, 124, 128, 134, 145, 167, 235, 238, 249, 260, 284, 286*
Poelcappelle, *48, 54, 57, 58, 87, 115, 123, 124, 148, 154, 169, 217, 286*
poison gas, *242*
Polygon Wood, *40, 44, 48, 58*

R

Ravebeek Creek, *57, 113, 141, 184, 185, 188, 189, 204, 211, 226, 245, 257, 260, 265, 276*
Rawlinson, Lieutenant General Sir Henry, *9, 34*

Red Line, *124, 134, 152, 154, 180, 184, 185, 188, 189, 201, 204, 207, 211, 214, 217, 218, 223, 226, 232*
regimental aid posts (RAP), *228*
Ribot, Alexandre, *13*
Richardson, Captain John, *201*
Rosenthal, Brigadier General Charles, *148, 150, 238, 240*
Rupprecht, Field Marshal Crown Prince, *286*
Russell, Major General Sir Andrew, *189, 194, 211, 214, 242*

S
Second World War, *27, 128, 194, 286*
shelling, *58, 65, 116, 134, 167, 174, 209, 245*
Small Box Respirator, *242*
S.S. 143, Instructions for the Training of Platoons for Offensive Action, *78*
standing barrage, *65*

Stokes 3.2-inch (81.2mm) trench mortar, *143, 161, 204*

T
Tiber Copse, *201*
training of 3rd Australian Division, *78, 84, 87, 89*
trench mortar, *100, 101, 113, 133, 143, 152, 161*
Tyne Cot Commonwealth War Graves Cemetery, *195*

U
U-boat operations, *21, 89, 282*

V
Verdun, *9, 13, 58, 89, 282*
Vindictive Crossroads, *268, 270*
von Falkenhayn, Field Marshal Eric, *89, 100, 113*
von Hindenburg, Field Marshal Paul, *100*
von Kuhl, General Herman, *54, 286*

W

withdrawal, *81, 145*
  9th Brigade, *217, 218, 223, 226*
  10th Brigade, *214, 217*
  decision pertaining to advance, hold or, *211, 214*
World War First, *276*
  Second, *27, 128, 194, 286*

Y

Ypres aerial view of, Cloth Hall, *254*
  First Battle of, *6, 9*
  topography of, *2*
Ypres Ridge, *30, 34*
Ypres—Roulers railway line, *174*

Z

Zonnebeke Road, *167, 169, 174, 257*

www.ingramcontent.com/pod-product-compliance
Lightning Source LLC
Chambersburg PA
CBHW011747220426
43667CB00020B/2928